D0836503

SPIRITFRUIT

THE GRACES OF THE SPIRIT-FILLED LIFE

SpiritFruit

THE GRACES OF THE SPIRIT-FILLED LIFE

JERRY • VINES

BROADMAN
&HOLMAN
PUBLISHERS

NASHVILLE, TENNESSEE

© 2001 by Jerry Vines
All rights reserved
Printed in the United States of America

0-8054-2397-4

Published by Broadman & Holman Publishers, Nashville, Tennessee

Dewey Decimal Classification: 234
Subject Heading: CHRISTIAN LIVING

Quotations from James Merritt are from his sermons found at Sermon Search by
One Pace: www.sermonsearch.com

Unless otherwise noted, Scripture quotations are from the Holy Bible, New
International Version, copyright © 1973, 1978, 1984 by International Bible
Society. Passages marked NASB are from the New American Standard Bible,
© the Lockman Foundation, 1960, 1962, 1963, 1968, 1971, 1972, 1973, 1975,
1977; used by permission. Passages marked The Message are from *The Message*, the
New Testament in Contemporary English, © 1993 by Eugene H. Peterson, published by NavPress, Colorado Springs, Colorado.

Library of Congress Cataloging-in-Publication Data

Vines, Jerry.
    SpiritFruit : the graces of the Spirit-filled life / by Jerry Vines.
        p.   cm.
    Includes bibliographical references.
    ISBN 0-8054-2397-4 (pbk.)
    1. Fruit of the Spirit. 2. Christian life—Baptist authors. I. Title: Spirit fruit.
    II. Title.
BV4501.2.V474 2000
234'.13—DC21

                                                                    00–057973
                                                                    CIP

2 3 4 5 05 04 03 02 01

CONTENTS

THE NEGLECTED FRUIT

Once upon a time there was a handsome and heroic prince. He had his eye on a young lady from the kingdom. He really liked her. He knew he had to travel abroad for quite a long time, so he asked one of his servants to tell the young lady about his love for her. "Show her how cool I am. Show her all my powers and stuff and please, please don't forget to show her some fruit from my beautiful orchard."

So the servant did just that. He attempted to impress the girl with the powers of his prince. He took her to the mountain of miracles and showed her some amazing sights. Then, he pointed to the sky to show her his prince's signs in the sky. Later, he showed her the well of wonders and pulled some incredible objects from it.

The young lady was certainly impressed. She considered giving her heart to the prince, but she always held back. The servant wondered how he might help her make the final decision to love his prince. Then he remembered what his prince had said. "Don't forget to show her some beautiful fruit in my orchard." Oh yes! The fruit! He had neglected the fruit. That's the ticket, he thought! I'll show her the fruit from the prince's orchard!

To be perfectly honest, the servant had not been out to the orchard for quite a long time. The gate was rusty. It creaked and squeaked as he opened it. The trees in the orchard were in desperate need of cultivation and pruning. Nevertheless, the servant found an unusual tree in the middle of the orchard. It was special because it yielded nine separate fruits, each one delicious and nutritious.

Well, the servant began picking the fruit. Soon, he had one of each of the nine fruits in a basket. He took the fruit to the young lady, and guess what . . . He finally won her heart for his prince.

You know, all of his incredible sights and powers were impressive. Yet she needed something more. The fruit satisfied her hunger, nourished her body, and met the deepest hungers of her life. At last, the prince had answered her lifelong questions.

In my previous books on the Holy Spirit, *SpiritLife* and *SpiritWorks*, I have discussed the person, work, and manifestations of the Holy Spirit. But I have come to the conviction that the most needed area in our understanding of the Holy Spirit is probably the most neglected one. I refer to the fruit of the Spirit as mentioned by Paul in Galatians 5:22–23. The fruit of the Spirit is certainly not so sensational or spectacular as the gifts of the Spirit. Producing the fruit of the Spirit involves a slower process. It requires a cultivation time. I touched on the fruit of the Spirit in a chapter in *SpiritWorks* entitled, "Got Fruit?" There I said, "The evidence of Christ's influence in a life is shown in the fruit that life produces. . . ." I continued, "The real, indisputable evidence that the Holy Spirit is working powerfully in me is that my life bears the fruit of the Spirit." That is the subject of the book you hold in your hands.

Often we think we can sweep people off by the glitter and glamour of spiritual gifts. But we may more often win people by the slow, steady, substantive fruit of the Spirit. Sometimes people may be awed by the fireworks of the faith, but I am of the conviction they are more often won by the fruit of the faith.

Acknowledgments

I want to thank Nancy Smith again for her help in making my language a bit more contemporary and conversational. She has been invaluable to me in these three books on the Holy Spirit.

Also, I want to thank Shirley Cannon, my secretary, who has faithfully worked on this manuscript as on the previous ones. Also, Jacki Raulerson has given excellent assistance.

I am indebted to my friends at Broadman & Holman Publishers for publishing the work and helping me toward its completion. Len Goss, my editor, is great. Also, thanks to Ken Stephens, Bucky Rosenbaum, John Landers, Kim Overcash, and Lisa Parnell.

I hope this third volume in my Holy Spirit trilogy will be as much a blessing to you as it was to me. I am sure all of us want to learn more about SpiritFruit!

*But the fruit of the Spirit is
love, joy, peace, patience, kindness, goodness,
faithfulness, gentleness and self-control.*
GALATIANS 5:22–23

CHAPTER 1

GOD AMONG THE ORCHARDS

T. DeWitt Talmadge was the colorful and creative pastor of the Brooklyn Tabernacle in New York in the late 1800s. His written sermons still show remarkable and entertaining content. His sermon "God Among the Orchards" fascinates readers with its tour of Bible orchards. We move from Adam's orchard in Eden, to Solomon's orchard in the Song of Solomon, to Pilate's orchard and the cross of Christ, until we reach the orchard in heaven. It makes me think of God's produce department.

Fruit! Do you love fruit? I really do. For a number of years our church staff has been sending to Janet and me a subscription to the Fruit of the Month Club for a Christmas gift. Each month we receive a different, delicious fruit. One month it's apples. Um, um! The next it is plums. Yum, yum! Then it is peaches. My, my! I love fruit.

My favorite section in the grocery store is the produce department—though I must admit the ice cream section is a close second! But there is something about the fruit in the produce section. The colors, the shapes, the sizes, the smells. The English word *fruit* comes from the Latin *frui*, which means "to enjoy or take pleasure in." What would life be without fruit? Fruit puts freshness and sweetness on our tables.

Paul, describing Christian character, uses the picture of fruit. Why? Well, fruit is the result on the outside of a tree of life on the inside. The fruit of the Spirit is the result of the work of the Holy Spirit on the inside of our lives. This is why sometimes we refer to the fruit of the Spirit as the "graces" of the Spirit. SpiritFruit is not the result of any work we do. Rather, it is the result, the outward expression, of the Holy Spirit's life at work within us.

Fruit does not grow naturally. Weeds grow naturally. The fruit of the Spirit grows supernaturally! That's what we are going to talk about in the chapters to follow. The Holy Spirit does a work in and through us, which is described in the Bible as the fruit of the Spirit.

Come with me now, and let's visit God among the orchards.

See the Orchard!

In my previous books on the Holy Spirit, I made a threefold distinction between the gift of the Spirit, the gifts of the Spirit, and the graces of the Spirit. Let's review each briefly.

The Gift of the Spirit

The Holy Spirit himself is called "the Gift." We read this in Acts 2:38: "Peter replied, 'Repent and be baptized, every one of you, in the name of Jesus Christ for the forgiveness of your sins. And you will receive the gift of the Holy Spirit.'"

The gift also refers to salvation itself. Remember the words of Jesus to the woman at the well? "Jesus answered her, 'If you knew the gift of God and who it is that asks you for a drink, you would have asked him and he would have given you living water'" (John 4:10).

The last part of Romans 6:23 says, "the gift of God is eternal life in Christ Jesus our Lord." Ephesians 2:8–9 makes salvation as a gift very clear, "For it is by grace you have been saved, through faith—and this not from yourselves, it is the gift of God—not by works, so that no one can boast."

Jesus promises the gift of the Holy Spirit. In John 7:39 he said, "By this he meant the Spirit, whom those who believed in him were later to receive. . . ." Also, in John 14:16 he promises, "And I will ask the Father, and he will give you another Counselor to be with you forever."

God is not an Indian-giver. In the first grade my friend Billy gave me his yo-yo. Man, was I excited! But the next day he had a change of heart and took it back. Was I let down! I remember accusing him—"Indian-giver!" When a person is saved, the Holy Spirit comes into his or her life. This gift of salvation of the Holy Spirit is never taken away.

Are there other places in the New Testament where this gift is mentioned? You bet! Romans 5:5 says, "And hope does not disappoint us, because God has poured out his love into our hearts by the Holy Spirit, whom he has given us." First Thessalonians 4:8 says, "Therefore, he who rejects this instruction does not reject man but God, who gives you his Holy Spirit." See, when we are saved, we receive the gift of the Holy Spirit, and Christ comes into our lives by faith. God the Father and God the Son, in the person of the Holy Spirit, then dwell in our lives. Now that's a gift! I recently received a mail offer to receive a book I wanted—free. But, as always, there was a catch. I had to subscribe to their book club, buy three books yearly, then receive the "free gift." This wasn't really a gift. But the Holy Spirit's presence in a Christian's life is a true gift, with no strings attached.

The Gifts and Graces of the Spirit

In my book *SpiritWorks* I said, "The gift of the Holy Spirit brings good things into our lives . . . the Giver brings gifts." The gifts of the Spirit enable us to serve the Lord and be a blessing to others. See, every Christian has one or more spiritual gifts. "Now to each one the manifestation of the Spirit is given for the common good" (1 Cor. 12:7). No Christian has all of the gifts. "Are all apostles? Are all prophets? Are all teachers? Do all work miracles? Do all have gifts of healing? Do all speak in tongues? Do all interpret?" (12:29–30). No! These gifts are divinely given. "All these are the work of one and the same Spirit, and he gives them to each one, just as he determines" (1 Cor. 12:11). The Holy Spirit does not give the gifts to us for our personal pleasure or as toys for our amusement.

They are tools to use in our lives. How? Well, the gifts should minister to others. The Holy Spirit energizes us to serve others with our gifts. "Now about spiritual gifts, brothers, I do not want you to be ignorant. You know that when you were pagans, somehow or other you were influenced and led astray to mute idols. Therefore I tell you that no one who is speaking by the Spirit of God says, 'Jesus be cursed,' and no one can say, 'Jesus is Lord,' except by the Holy Spirit. There are different kinds of gifts, but the same Spirit" (1 Cor. 12:1–4).

What does "the fruit of the Spirit" really mean? First, the fruit of the Spirit represents traits of Christian character produced by the Holy Spirit in the life of a believer. See, this fruit reflects spiritual qualities in the personality and relationships of a Christian. It is these spiritual traits or reflections of personality in interpersonal relationships that Paul names "the fruit of the Spirit."

Sometimes these graces of character are pushed to the back of the bus, so to speak. The current emphasis on gifts is valid but can be out of proportion. Hey, the gifts are exciting. The graces may not be as high-end in the energy department. Miracles make headlines more than the grace of being patient. Casting out devils does grab more press than displaying gentleness in relationships. No top story there. Perhaps the gifts seem like "de bomb" these days and the graces don't. Right!

But, wait a minute! Maybe the fruit of the Spirit is neglected in today's culture, but not so in the Bible. For instance, think about love. It's the first grace mentioned. In 1 Corinthians 12:31 Paul says, "But eagerly desire the greater gifts." Then he moves into the beautiful thirteenth chapter, which is the great love chapter in the Bible. Love is not pushed to the back seat with Paul.

Remember those comparison/contrast essays in English class? Well, let's compare and contrast the gifts and graces of the Holy Spirit. The gifts have to do with power; graces have to do with character. Gifts point to what we *do*. Graces point to who we *are*. Gifts deal with action and graces deal with being.

Does possession of one or more spiritual gifts mean a Christian is spiritual? Think about it. The evidence of spirituality is primarily moral and ethical. Is your life Christlike? People are not likely to believe you are "in the Spirit" unless they see the fruit of the Spirit in you! Call it FruitVision for the Christian. A multimedia technological experience for believers! Just kidding!

The gifts and the graces of the Holy Spirit belong together. They complete the Christian. If Christians had graces without gifts, they would lack power. If Christians possessed gifts without graces, they would lack character. We need the gifts of the Spirit to serve effectively. We need the graces of the Spirit to live effectively.

The fruit of the Spirit keeps the gifts from becoming disruptive. Christians can exercise spiritual gifts in unloving and difficult ways. Have you ever met a gifted preacher who was offensive and ornery in his behavior? What was missing? The fruit of the Spirit.

Survey the Orchard!

Fruit is mentioned often in the Bible, both in the Old Testament and in the New Testament. It is used in two primary ways: sometimes fruit is referred to literally and sometimes figuratively. The Bible refers to trees (Matt. 12:33), vines (Matt. 21:33–34), and fields (Luke 12:16–17). Genesis 1:11 offers the first literal mention of fruit. On the third day of creation God said, "'Let the land produce vegetation . . . bear fruit with seed in it, according to their various kinds.' And it was so."

Think about this. God created fruit before man, therefore, for man's consumption. The word *fruit* means "to enjoy or to take pleasure in." The earth was uniquely designed for an inhabitant. Everything needed to sustain life was included in its creation. From the beginning, God prepared the earth for man. Obviously, man needs food; so before man was created, God made fruit.

Remember the "after his kind" from Genesis 1:1? Well, this is a hurdle that evolution theory has never been able to leap. God establishes the principle here that fruit will always produce according to the nature of its tree.

This principle is foundational to the science of genetics. When Darwin set forth his theory of evolution, he knew very little about the nature of the cell and did not know about genetics as we do. Now we know that the basic genetic structure of fruit does not change. Of course, we see mutations everywhere (in science this is referred to as microevolution). This means there is infinite variety among species of fruit. Did you know, for example, there are over 7,500 varieties of apples worldwide? There are apples of all shapes, colors, and tastes.[1] So, what does that mean? It means when you pluck fruit from an apple tree, you'll pick an apple, not a watermelon! See, what is true physically is also true spiritually. Spiritual fruit will always be consistent with the nature of its producer—the Holy Spirit.

Fruit is also mentioned in a figurative sense. Sometimes children are called fruit: " . . . that of the fruit of his loins, according to the flesh . . ." (Acts 2:30 KJV). We read about the fruit of the womb, " . . . Blessed art thou among women, and blessed is the fruit of thy womb (Luke 1:42 KJV). Even "the consequences of an action are described as its fruit."[2] So, in the figurative sense, fruit means "that which originates or comes from something." In other words, it is a result or an effect or a consequence. An "A" on your term paper is the "fruit" of your thorough research and careful writing.

Paul uses the word *fruit* in this way in Galatians 5:22. The *Dictionary of Pentecostal and Charismatic Movement* says, "The fruit of the Spirit is a figurative expression . . . to connect the behavior he advocates with the Holy Spirit."[3]

What about the Old Testament? God called the nation of Israel to a fruitful life. Israel was referred to as the olive, the fig, and the grape (see Judg. 9:7–15). The great tragedy is that Israel became an empty, fruitless vine (see Hos. 10:1; Isa. 5:1–7; Jer. 2:21). In the Old Testament, individual believers are called "trees of righteousness, the planting of the Lord" (Isa. 61:3 KJV). The Old Testament gives some hints of the New Testament presentation of a Spirit-controlled life as fruit. We see this in Psalm 1:3: "He is like a tree planted by streams of water, / which yields its fruit in season / and whose leaf does not wither. / Whatever he does prospers." Another verse promises, "They will still bear fruit in old age, . . ." (Ps. 92:14).

We see the figurative use of fruit in the New Testament. Jesus calls himself the "true vine" (John 15:1). In contrast to Israel, which failed to bear fruit, Jesus says he is the "true vine," and he produces fruit. Our communion with Jesus results in a life that bears spiritual fruit. There are other figurative uses of the word *fruit*. Sometimes fruit is used as a picture of sanctification, the progressive growth in righteousness of the believer. Romans 6:22 says, " . . . the benefit you reap leads to holiness, . . ."

We are also told that in heaven there will be a tree of life that will yield fruit every month of the year (Rev. 22:2). Now that's what I call a "Fruit of the Month Club!" Whether or not this tree will be literal, we know that in heaven there will be perpetual, eternal freshness and nourishment.

Sample the Orchard!

Is the fruit of a Christian another Christian, or is it the fruit of the Spirit? What gives? Both describe the fruit of the Spirit. Fruit is used in several ways in the New Testament to explain various behaviors and expressions of the Christian life.

As one example, giving is described as a fruit. "For Macedonia and Achaia were pleased to make a contribution for the poor among the saints in Jerusalem. They were pleased to do it, and indeed they owe it to them. For if the Gentiles have shared in the Jews' spiritual blessings, they owe it to the Jews to share with them their material blessings. So after I have completed this task and have made sure that they have received this fruit, I will go to Spain" (Rom. 15:26–28a). "Moreover, as you Philippians know, in the early days of your acquaintance with the gospel, when I set out from Macedonia, not one church shared with me in the matter of giving and receiving, except you only; for even when I was in Thessalonica, you sent me aid again and again when I was in need. Not that I am looking for a gift, but I am looking for what may be credited to your account" (Phil. 4:15–17). These gifts are described as fruit. Get this, fruit is the result on the outside of your life of what is on the inside. Christian giving should result from our growing love relationship with Christ.

Our praise to the Lord is also an example of fruit. "Through Jesus, therefore, let us continually offer to God a sacrifice of praise—the fruit of lips that confess his name" (Heb. 13:15). But remember, fruit is the result on the outside of life of what is on the inside. Our expressions of praise should be consistent and the natural result of a growing relationship with Christ on the inside. A young Christian, growing in her understanding of God's work of grace in her life, sings the hymn "Amazing Grace" with a greater sense of praise.

What else is considered fruit? People won to Christ are described as fruit. Romans 1:13 says, ". . . that I planned many times to come to you . . . in order that I might have a harvest among you, just as I have had among the other Gentiles." Philippians 1:22 says, "If I am to go on living in the body, this will mean fruitful labor for me. Yet what shall I choose? I do not know!" Look at John 4:36: "Even now the reaper draws his wages, even now he harvests the crop for eternal life, so that the sower and the reaper may be glad together." But remember, fruit is the result on the outside of life on the inside. Witnessing is not something that can be forced. Winning people to Christ should be a natural output of the growing relationship the believer has with Jesus Christ on the inside.

Finally, the traits of Christian character in Galatians 5:22–23 are described as fruit. Remember? The fruit of the Spirit represent the traits of Christian character produced by the Holy Spirit in the life of a believer. This is where it's at! This is the Christian personality as it is intended to be, making full use of God's guidelines for Christians as they live and relate to one another.

According to Jesus, the test of any life is its fruit. Just as trees and plants are identified by what they produce, Jesus says people are known by the fruit their lives produce.

Consider Matthew 7:15–20:

"Watch out for false prophets. They come to you in sheep's clothing, but inwardly they are ferocious wolves. By their fruit you will recognize them. Do people pick grapes from thornbushes, or figs from thistles? Likewise every good tree bears good fruit, but a bad tree bears bad fruit. A good tree cannot bear bad fruit, and a bad tree cannot bear good fruit. Every tree that does not bear good fruit is cut down and thrown into the fire. Thus, by their fruit you will recognize them."

Look at the context. Note verses 21–23 following Jesus' remarks on fruit.

"Not everyone who says to me, 'Lord, Lord,' will enter the kingdom of heaven, but only he who does the will of my Father who is in heaven. Many will say to me on that day, 'Lord, Lord, did we not prophesy in your name, and in your name drive out demons and perform many miracles?' Then I will tell them plainly, 'I never knew you. Away from me, you evildoers!'"

Let's reread what Jesus said about fruit. He didn't ask us to examine Christians for signs and wonders or great prophetic gifts. He said, "Ye shall know them by their fruits" (Matt. 7:16 KJV). Simple, isn't it? Hey, this doesn't mean the miracles are minimized, but it does put the focus where it should be. We do not gauge spirituality or Christianity by the spectacular or the sensational, even though our *Inside Edition* or *Hard Copy* world might make us think so. Remember, the gifts can be imitated by Satan and they will be, but Satan cannot imitate the fruit of the Spirit (see 2 Thess. 2:9; Rev. 13).

Jesus is looking for fruit! Remember the striking parable in Luke 13:6–9? The search was for fruit. Is this why some Christians take an early, sudden trip to heaven? Is it possible that you and I may be under a one-year cultivation program? Has the Lord decided he will give you one more year to let a Sunday School teacher work on you? One more year so that your mate can try to cultivate some fruit in your life? Just one more year to allow a pastor to cultivate your life? One more year to see if all this cultivation can squeeze one little fig out of your life or mine?

Now, think about the parable I gave you in the preface. What attracted the lovely young maiden to the prince? Not the miracles. The fruit! As you survey God's Bible Orchard, don't neglect the fruit!

Do you want an exciting and vital Christian life? Do you want God to use you to bring others to himself? Then, you need fruit. You need the Holy Spirit to produce the fruit in your life.

Want to know more? Read the rest of this book to learn more about how the Holy Spirit can turn your life into one of God's orchards.

CHAPTER 2

IS THERE A POMOLOGIST IN THE HOUSE?

Did you ever study Greek and Roman myths in school? I did. Do you remember Zeus and Medusa? How about Narcissus? Myths are really a way to explain the unexplainable in human life. Before Christianity, many people put their faith in mythical gods and goddesses and their supposed supernatural works.

Do you remember Pomona, the Roman goddess of fruit? I bet you don't. I didn't. I found out about her while doing research on the Internet. I was going through several references for fruit. I wound up at the West Virginia University Department of Pomology Web site. What's pomology? Well, the word *pomology* comes from the same goddess Pomona. So pomology is the science of fruit growing, and a pomologist is one who studies fruit growing.

Think of Paul in the Bible. In Galatians, he discusses spiritual fruit and how we can grow it in our lives. Picture Paul holding up a Bible fruit tree with both arms, shaking it, and causing fruit to come falling down. He gathers the fruit in the basket of Galatians 5 and shouts, "Here it is! The fruit of the Spirit is . . . ."

So I think Paul could be our Bible pomologist. He helps us learn more about the Holy Spirit and the SpiritFruit our Christian lives can show.

Paul's guidance leads us to grow the fruit in our own lives. Real fruit is not only beautiful but also nutritious. Spiritual fruit is too, when blooming in the lives of believers. You know, there is a pomologist in the house, and his name is Paul.

You may wonder if the Book of Galatians says much about the Holy Spirit. You bet! Scattered throughout this small book are numerous references to the Holy Spirit. Remember our division of the truth about the Spirit? Basically, we have the gift of the Spirit (salvation), the gifts of the Spirit (service), and the graces of the Spirit (sanctification). Do we find all three areas in Galatians? Absolutely!

Paul describes the gift of the Spirit in Galatians. He talks about being born after the Spirit (4:29). He also mentions receiving the Spirit (3:2, 14). Paul clearly points out that we begin the Christian life in the Spirit (3:3) and are to live in the Spirit (5:25). He further says that the Holy Spirit has been sent into our hearts to enable us to call God our Father (4:6). Paul also says that we, through the Spirit, wait for the hope of righteousness by faith (5:5).

Paul asks, if we commence the Christian life by the Holy Spirit, why should we attempt to live the Christian life in any other way (3:3)? So he encourages us to be led of the Spirit (5:18), and then he commands us to walk in the Spirit (5:16, 25).

What about the "gifts of the Spirit"? He doesn't really say much about that; I can find only one reference to the "gifts of the Spirit." In Galatians 3:5 he indicates that the heavenly Father ministered or supplied miracles to the Galatian believers by the Spirit. That's all, folks! The gifts aren't Paul's focus here.

Paul also discusses the "graces of the Spirit" in Galatians 5:22–23. He begins with a series of statements that contrasts living the Christian life in the flesh (in the strength of the old nature) with living in the Spirit (living the Christian life by the power of the indwelling Spirit). "Live by the Spirit, and you will not gratify the desires of the sinful nature" (5:16). Then Paul explains that the flesh and the Spirit are in a battle with each other: "For the sinful nature desires what is contrary to the Spirit, and the Spirit what is contrary to the sinful nature. They are in conflict with each other, so that you do not do what you want" (5:17). In chapter 6 he warns us to emphasize the Spirit, not the flesh: "The one who sows to please his sinful nature, from that nature will reap destruction; the one who sows to please the Spirit, from the Spirit will reap eternal life" (Gal. 6:8). What's the point? Our flesh (the old nature) can never produce spiritual life. Spiritual life can only be produced by the Holy Spirit. This is the context Paul provides to discuss the fruit of the Spirit.

In Galatians 5, Paul contrasts the "works of the flesh" in verse 19 with the "fruit of the Spirit" in verse 22. Seventeen works of the flesh are scattered on the page. Actually, this is just one list; there are others in the New Testament (see 1 Cor. 6:9–11; Rom. 1:28–32). These passages show just how deadly sin is. The words describe how sin manifests itself in our lives. I don't want to go there. Let's just say that this is sin's vocabulary in its unending, monstrous reality. To read this list is like a late-night viewing of *The Rocky Horror Picture Show*. Our old nature is shown in all its foul, putrid manifestations. These dreaded behaviors produce chaotic, confused, and disruptive results. Just look at all the messed up lives around you!

But! What a contrast! Look at verse 22! "But the fruit of the Spirit is love, joy, peace, patience, kindness, goodness, faithfulness." The fruit of the

Spirit is not manufactured by machine. Fruit is produced. Fruit is the result on the outside of the life lived on the inside. Paul shows us the result of the Spirit operating in the life of a believer.

The word *fruit* is singular, not plural. Why? Well, in Paul's garden nine fruits grow. Drescher says, "In it grows the honeysuckle of love, the rose of joy, the lily of peace, the snowdrop of longsuffering [patience], the mignonette of kindliness, the daisy of goodness, the forget-me-not of faithfulness, the violet of meekness and the wall-flower of self-control."[1]

Others say *fruit* is singular because love is the one fruit Paul emphasizes. According to this view, love exists in eight expressions. Still others point out that the nine nouns can be arranged in groups of three, symbolizing the threefold relationship of the Christian life. The first three point to our God-ward relationship, the next three to our man-ward relationships, and the last three to our self-ward relationship.

An observation of nature shows that fruit comes in four categories. Pomes have cores and small seeds; apples and pears are pomes. Drupes contain a single pit; peaches and plums fall into this category. Then there are berries, such as strawberries and raspberries. Then some fruit is in the category of aggregates—they grow in clusters, like bananas or dates.

The fruit of the Spirit is a cluster. To me, the singular fruit refers to the unified, harmonious character the Holy Spirit produces in a Christian life. Here is the life of the Spirit in all its fullness. The fruit of the Spirit gives beauty, richness, balance, and order to the Christian life.

This also seems to indicate that the graces of the Christian life derive from one source, the Holy Spirit. The works of the flesh are separate acts that people commit. The ninefold fruit of the Holy Spirit, by contrast, is the sum of SpiritLife working from the inside out in the believer. Henry Barclay Swete says, "The use of the singular points to the unity of the character which the Spirit creates."[2] In other words, the fruit is shown through the supernatural made practical in our daily lives.

All nine graces are to be seen as a whole in every Christian's life. A Christian can't say, "I'm into joy, but not meekness." Or, "I'm a self-controlled Christian, but I'm not much of a kindness Christian." We are to display every fragrance and flavor of the fruit of the Holy Spirit.

Each of these graces should work with the others. Have you ever seen someone try to be patient without love? A person showing that sort of patience can be hateful, overbearing, and guilt-producing. All the graces are to be a composite in the life of the believer who yields to the indwelling Holy Spirit.

Remember Bible pomology? Some specific words will help us understand how the fruit of the Spirit is to be displayed in the life of a believer. These words summarize the spiritual fruit-bearing process.

Planting

Logic tells us there must first be planting to yield fruit. In your life and in mine the seed of the Word must be planted in the soil of our hearts. Jesus used this picture several times (see Matt. 13:3–9; Mark 4:3–9; Luke 8:4–8). He specifically said that "the seed is the Word of God" (Luke 8:11). The same picture is presented in James 1:21, "Therefore, get rid of all moral filth and the evil that is so prevalent and humbly accept the word planted in you, which can save you." When the seed of the Word is received in the human heart by faith, life begins. Hey, fruit doesn't grow on a dead tree. W. A. Criswell says, "Dead posts produce no fruit. Those beautiful graces cannot be outwardly hung upon a tree like toys and ornaments upon a Christmas tree. Fruitage in the Spirit requires rootage in the Spirit."[3]

The fruit of the Spirit is not the result of natural generation but of *supernatural* generation. It's a wonderful miracle when a person comes to Christ and receives the Holy Spirit. New characteristics and behaviors begin to show up in a life just as pears, apples, and grapes show up in an orchard or on vines. Picture a man who has received Christ as Savior. He begins to talk sweetly to his wife. What a change! He is tender toward his children. During the day he hums melodies. He might even let out a *hallelujah* along the way. He has joy and peace in his life. Instead of chewing out a bungling clerk, he smiles and waits with a patience not true to his old nature. New traits begin to appear in his life like new fruit on a tree.

These graces of character aren't developed from our own efforts. Our efforts only produce cheap imitations of the real thing. Have you ever seen anyone try to be patient in his or her own power? The result is strained, forced, and ineffective behavior. Or have you ever seen anyone attempt to mimic Holy Spirit joy? About all you see is a forced smile and a coaxing voice. What about Holy Spirit love? If someone tries to show this without the Holy Spirit, the result is shallow sentimentalism.

Obviously, we don't become God's child without the Holy Spirit. We also can't live the life of God's child without the Holy Spirit. Galatians 3:3 says, "Are you so foolish? After beginning with the Spirit, are you now trying to attain your goal by human effort?" The Holy Spirit is the source of life and power necessary to correct a Christian's behavior. Fruit results from a long-living process. The process is complex and intricate. Germination and growth are not instant. The process is a gradual, growing one.

Fruit is not engineered or designed. We don't draft fruit blueprints on a drawing board, then send them to a factory for production. Nor can spiritual fruit be designed and assembled like a computer chip. Spiritual fruit results from life created on the inside by the Holy Spirit.

Growing fruit is not a noisy, sensational process. No one says, "Call *Inside Edition*! Fruit is growing!" No, fruit grows when buds appear. The fruit's flower produces a fragrance. The fruit grows and ripens. What is the evidence that the fruit of the Spirit is growing in a Christian or in a Christian church? Is it singing, shouting, and outward exuberance in a church service? Not necessarily. A better indication could be improvements in the church members' relationships with one another. Perhaps members begin relating to each other in love. Or they may demonstrate kindness or reliability in their relationships with one another. This slow process of manifesting the fruit is the best proof of growth.

Cultivating

Fruit growing also includes the process of cultivation. Once the seed is planted and growth begins, good cultivation is essential. A nourishing environment is vital. Rich soil, plenty of water, and bright sunshine are needed to produce abundant fruit.

Let's talk facts. Sixteen elements are necessary for the growth of real fruit. Three come from water and air (carbon, hydrogen, oxygen). The other thirteen are absorbed from the soil, primarily nitrogen, phosphorous, and potassium.[4]

Location! Location! Location! The location of fruit trees and bushes is very important. They should be located in direct sunlight. The soil needs to be rich and full of nutrients. Alkalinity and acidity in the soil must be balanced for ideal growth.

This is also true for growing the fruit of the Spirit. Spiritual fruit grows best when located in the presence of the "Son." Daily fellowship and relationship with Jesus is absolutely essential for growth of spiritual fruit.

See, fruit of the Spirit is not something we can produce ourselves. It is the fruit of the *Spirit*, not the fruit of the Christian. But, hey, this is not an excuse for us to relax. The Bible teaches we should cooperate with the Holy Spirit as He cultivates these graces in us.

This is why many graces of the Spirit are commanded of believers in various places in the Bible. We are commanded to love, to be patient, and to be faithful. What's going on with that? Well, figures of speech can't be pressed too far. For instance, a football coach says his running back is a thoroughbred. What does he mean? Well, he doesn't mean he eats oats and runs on racetracks. He just means his running back is the best of the best. Don't push figures of speech in the Bible to extremes.

Obviously, we can't "command" fruit to grow, but we should have a degree of involvement. Second Peter 1:5 says, "For this very reason, make every effort to add to your faith goodness; and to goodness, knowledge." Then, verse 8 says, "For if you possess these qualities in increasing measure, they will keep you from being ineffective and unproductive in your knowledge of our Lord Jesus Christ." We must obey and cooperate with the Holy Spirit. Strauss says, "The operation of the Spirit in the believer demands the cooperation of the believer himself."[5]

Here's how it works. As we read the Bible's commands concerning the fruit of the Spirit, we try to obey them. Excuse me? What's this? We can't! Whoa! This drives us to God in prayer. Deal with it! We confess our failures and surrender to the control of the Holy Spirit. We then allow him to produce his fruit in us. So the Holy Spirit produces the fruit as we bear it.

The nine graces are produced by the Holy Spirit only by our permission. The fruit of the Spirit is the result of his life in us and our response to him. As we allow the Holy Spirit's power in our lives and if we obey his commands, he is released to work his miracles of character in our lives.

Cultivating fruit also involves *pruning*. Say what? Pruning? Sounds kind of radical, doesn't it? Hold on. Pruning takes time, energy, and a great deal of skill. Careful training is required to learn when, where, and how to prune fruit. A skilled pruner learns to make good cuts with sharp tools. It's like getting a haircut, but with leaves instead! But pruning is essential. It results in growth and higher fruit production. An ignorant, unskilled pruner can do major damage. (Just like a bad haircut! Ladies, do you know what I mean?)

But, hold on! I have good news for you! We have a Master Pruner! Jesus says, "'. . . my Father is the gardener. He cuts off every branch in me that bears no fruit, while every branch that does bear fruit he prunes so that it will be even more fruitful'" (John 15:1–2). Our Heavenly Father is the one who prunes us. He knows when, where, and how to do the job.

A good pruner uses two kinds of tools. There are the light pruning shears and the heavy-duty loppers. Our Master Pruner has shears—the Word of God (John 15:2–3)! Hebrews 4:12 says, "For the word of God is living and active. Sharper than any double-edged sword, it penetrates even to dividing soul and spirit, joints and marrow; it judges the thoughts and attitudes of the heart." The Lord clips away the obnoxious branches and dead leaves of the old life. This frees us to let the new fruit of the Spirit grow better in our lives.

Sometimes, however, it's time for the loppers. Heavy-duty stuff. What's that? Discipline! Hebrews 12:11 says, "No discipline seems pleasant at the time, but painful. Later on, however, it produces a harvest of righteousness and peace for those who have been trained by it." At times we let big areas of sin hang out in our lives. When we refuse to respond to the Bible shears, the Lord uses the lopper of discipline. But it draws us closer to him and makes us more fruitful.

Think about it. Unpruned plants bear some fruit. But as the *Taylor's Guide* says, "Well-pruned plants will almost always bear bigger crops of larger, less-blemished fruit."[6] That statement sounds like it's right out of John 15!

Producing

The third step in the fruit-growing process is production. Planting has taken place. Cultivation is completed. Now it is production time.

There are two purposes for fruit once it is produced. The first purpose is consumption and the second is propagation.

Consumption

Fruit is produced to be eaten. It has food value and is intended to provide nourishment. Fruit doesn't produce fruit for itself. Apple trees don't eat their own apples.

Americans eat a great deal of fruit. In the mid-1980s, our total fruit consumption was more than two hundred pounds per person per year.[7]

Just as an apple tree doesn't eat its own apples, Christians don't bear the fruit of the Spirit for themselves. SpiritFruit is produced to feed others. People all around us are starving for love, joy, peace. . . . It's obvious they are hungry for SpiritFruit. Where will they get this spiritual nourishment if not from people who know Christ? We are to provide nourishment for others.

Have you thanked God for fruit lately? Have you thanked God for the acid in fruit, which keeps our dinner table from being tasteless? Or how long since you thanked God for the sweets in fruit, which keep our tables from being too sour? Have you ever thanked God for the fruit of the Spirit? Their acids keep our Christian life from being dull and insipid. The sweets of SpiritFruit keep our lives from being too sour.

Fruit is really cool. Did you know that fruit provides all the vitamins, minerals, natural sugars, and amino acids needed for human nutrition? What's the big deal? Natural acids are necessary for prompt elimination of toxins, poisonous acids, and other impurities produced by internal sources like digestion and metabolism. Also, these acids help destroy impurities from external sources such as air, water, or pesticides.[8] Fruit protects us against cancer, heart disease, and stroke.[9] Eating fruit makes sense!

Galatians 5 focuses on Bible pomology. The Bible's teachings about fruit are crystallized in nine words! It's as if Paul holds up a Bible fruit tree with both arms, shakes it, and causes the fruit to come falling down. He gathers the fruit in the basket of Galatians 5 and shouts, "Hey, the fruit of the Spirit is . . . !"

The fruit of the Spirit is cool too! It provides the necessary ingredients needed for human relations. This SpiritFruit helps people eliminate toxins and poisons like anger and bitterness or resentment and rebellion in the heart.

Take a look at your life. Is it attractive? Is it appealing? Is it appetizing to others? Think for a moment what a home would be like if the fruit of the Spirit were present. Picture a home with love, joy, and peace. Then picture the happiness that patience, kindness, and goodness would bring. The home can be even stronger if it is characterized by faith, gentleness, and self-control.

The fruit of the Spirit certainly can make a difference at church! Talk about relationships! The nine graces of the Spirit make the difference in the classroom, on the job, or in our social life. Showing love in these relationships is like eating a sweet apple. Demonstrating kindness in these areas of life is like enjoying a tasty plum!

Propagation

There is a second purpose for the production of fruit, and it is propagation. Seeds in fruit make more fruit possible. Remember that fruit produces "after its kind." We plant the seeds of the fruit of the Spirit so others will come to Jesus Christ. Actually, the fruit of the Spirit makes us like Christ. And by planting seeds, we draw others to Christ.

Drawing others to Christ involves witnessing. How? By opening our mouths and speaking the good news of the gospel. But the witness of our lips must be made credible by the witness of our lives.

A man was brought to Christ by another man who worked beside him on the job. He said, "He never said a word. But the beauty of his life convinced me I needed something he had." Our lives are to have the fragrance and taste of Christ. Dr. Paul Brand says that people are to "taste the flavor of Jesus through contact with you."[10]

People need these spiritual character traits in their lives. Hey, most of us realize we need love. Most of us probably see the need to be kinder.

Wouldn't you like to be considered more dependable? I know I would. When unsaved people see these character traits in us, they realize their own need. It should also create in them a desire to know the same Savior who helps us live with these characteristics.

John 15 discusses fruit growing. This passage is "de bomb." In other words, it is remarkable. It is the night before his death on the cross. In just a few hours he will die on the cross for the sins of the world. Like a seed, he will be planted in the soil of Calvary. When he, the seed, dies, he will make life possible for millions. Jesus is sharing his final words with his disciples. He has been teaching them that the Holy Spirit will be coming to live inside them. In that setting, Jesus gives the remarkable teaching of John 15.

Perhaps Jesus was walking with the disciples that night from the upper room to the garden of Gethsemane and saw a vineyard along the way. Picture great clusters of grapes on the branches of the vines. It's all about fruit. In this passage Jesus uses the word *fruit* seven times. He reminds the disciples that he is the "true vine" and that the heavenly Father is "the gardener." He also clearly points out to them that they are branches.

Jesus couldn't be clearer. Think about it. Branches don't produce the fruit. The vine does. The branches simply bear the fruit. Christians don't produce spiritual fruit. Jesus does. Our job is to bear the fruit he produces.

It's all about being connected. Jesus taught that fruit results from the branches' connection with the vine. In the King James Version, Jesus uses the word *abide* nine times in this passage. That's probably a word you use every day. Yeah, right! It means "to dwell or to remain in." It means "to stay close, to maintain heart communion" with Jesus; and it is the secret of Bible pomology. We don't produce the fruit. We just bear it.

As we maintain heart communion with Jesus, there will be a development in fruit-bearing. Look at the progression: Fruit . . . more fruit (v. 2), "much fruit" (v. 8), "fruit that will last" (v. 16)! I'd say that's a big-time crop!

An exhibition was opened in England by the queen. She was making a tour of the various presentations. She found one exhibitor slouched in his chair, sound asleep. Everyone watched to see how the queen would react. She paused a moment, then smiled. She went on to the next exhibit. Why? Because royalty does not force itself on anyone. Nor does God's Spirit. He produces his fruit where he is invited to work. As we yield to the Holy Spirit, he produces his fruit in us.

Yes, there's a pomologist in the house. Paul gives us a plan for planting, cultivating, and producing SpiritFruit in our lives as Christians.

Remember Pomona, the Roman goddess of fruit? Let's tell her to "get out of the house!" She's just a myth. But Paul provides the guidelines we need. He's the man with the plan! He's our pomologist, and he's in the house!

CHAPTER 3

LOVE APPLES

Apples! What's better and sweeter than an apple! There are over 7,200 varieties of apples worldwide. They come in all shapes, sizes, colors and tastes—the delectable Golden Delicious, the magnificent Liberty, the Northern Spy, the luscious Winesap. How tasty are apples!

Apples are prominent in mythological history. Aphrodite, goddess of love, is pictured with an apple in hand. The Trojan War was attributed to the "apple of discord." This golden apple was thrown down in the assembly of the gods by Eris, goddess of hate, thus precipitating the war. In the early American colonies, every farm had an orchard. So important were apple orchards that the first law passed prescribed a "proper punishment" for anyone robbing an apple orchard.

Apples spread across America, thanks to an itinerant preacher who was also an accomplished nurseryman. His name was John Chapman, but we know him as Johnny Appleseed. Rather eccentric, he walked barefooted wearing a mush hat, a burlap shirt, and ragged trousers. He scattered apple seeds, sold them, gave them away, and planted them up and down the Ohio River Valley, turning large parts of the early frontier into apple orchards.[1]

Apples have many health benefits. They reactivate beneficial intestinal bacteria. Their fibrous, juicy, nonsticky nature helps clean our teeth and exercise our gums. Apples remove impurities from the liver and inhibit the growth of disease-producing bacteria in the digestive tract. Eaten daily, apples can help prevent skin diseases, arthritis, and even liver problems.[2] The old adage "An apple a day keeps the doctor away" is indeed true. We know apples are ripening when the skin takes on color. We don't know for sure until we bite into one.

Love! What is sweeter and better than love? Paul scatters the sweet fragrance of love throughout Galatians. "I have been crucified with Christ and I no longer live, but Christ lives in me. The life I live in the body, I live by faith in the Son of God, who loved me and gave himself for me" (2:20). "For in Christ Jesus neither circumcision nor uncircumcision has any value. The only thing that counts is faith expressing itself through love" (5:6). "You, my brothers, were called to be free. But do not use your freedom to indulge the sinful nature; rather, serve one another in love" (5:13). "The entire law is summed up in a single command: 'Love your neighbor as yourself'" (5:14).

Then Paul places love at the head of the list of the SpiritFruit in Galatians 5:22. Love is the primary grace of the Christian life. It is the fountain from which all other graces flow. He installs it as the chief virtue of the Christian life (5:13–14). Jesus declared the supremacy of love when he said we are to love the Lord and to love our neighbor. As we have seen, Paul summarizes the whole law in this one word *love*. For a believer, love is

- a new constraint, "For Christ's love compels us, because we are convinced that one died for all, and therefore all died" (2 Cor. 5:14);
- a new covering, "Above all, love each other deeply, because love covers over a multitude of sins" (1 Pet. 4:8);
- a new commandment, "A new command I give you: Love one another. As I have loved you, so you must love one another" (John 13:34); and
- a new clothing, "And over all these virtues put on love, which binds them all together in perfect unity" (Col. 3:14).

Love means different things to different people. There is the heart-fluttering, breath-taking "love" of adolescence, filled with feelings and goose bumps. I have a little poem I like to use with our kids at church (usually met with a grimace or groan from them after I finish).

Love is a very funny thing,
It's shaped just like a lizard.
It wraps its tail around your throat
and goes right through your gizzard!

People "love" all kinds of things. "I love my Volvo." "I love peanut butter." "I love my dog." I heard about a bumper sticker on a pickup truck which said, "Wanted, prospective wife who loves dogs. Send picture of dog." Nah. Don't think he'll have any beauties primping for him. Love is often determined by context, don't you think?

SpiritFruit love is completely different from these other kinds of love. It is not merely a human emotion, for it is of divine origin. First John 4:7–8 says, "Beloved, let us love one another: for love is of God . . . for God is love" (KJV). When we receive Christ as personal Savior, the Holy Spirit pours God's love into our hearts (Rom. 5:5). Now we have within us a supernatural trait, the divine love of God. We are now capable of expressing love in our relationships with other people.

Have you ever noticed that people young and old are starving for love? Madalyn Murray O'Hair vanished in 1995. Though she has not been found, her diaries have been recovered. They make for very sad reading. She talks about her money problems and her desire for power and political office, and she pleads for love. Her diaries often cry, "Somebody, somewhere, love me!" This woman, obnoxious to many, was literally starving for love.

What does love have to do with Christianity or with God or with you or me? Rock diva Tina Turner's song asked that question a few years ago—"What's love got to do with it?" Kind of a cynical take on that "second-hand emotion," wouldn't you say? Yet it seems many people agree with her, and few have experienced the spiritual quality of love. Why? Probably because few Christians are reflecting SpiritFruit love in their personalities and relationships with others.

Love Defined

The word *love* is used often in the Bible. Paul really uses it. In the Greek language there are three primary words for love. *Eros* means "sensual love." It has to do more with a lustful relationship. This word is so offensive that it is not found planted one time in the sweet soil of Scripture. There is another level of love, *philos*, which is social in nature. The words *Philadelphia* and *philanthropy* come from this word. It refers to the warm love we feel for family and friends. But the word Paul uses in this SpiritFruit passage is *agape*, spiritual love. This is high-level love. This love is divine in origin.

Love is a noun and also a verb. Paul uses the noun form seventy-five times and the verb form thirty-four times. How's that, English teachers? As a noun it refers to unconquerable benevolence or kindness. It seeks the highest good for others, regardless of their treatment of us. Barclay says, "Agape is the spirit in the heart that will never seek anything but the highest good of its fellow persons."[3]

Love is also a verb. To love results from a decision to do the best for another person. *Agape* love involves the mind as well as the heart. So it is not just a matter of emotions, or a "second-hand emotion," as many people think. We talk about "falling in love" like falling into a tub of chocolate pudding. But think about it, love is a deed before it is a feeling. Feelings follow, but the will is involved first. Again Barclay says *agape* is "the deliberate effort—only made with the help of God—to never seek anything but the best for others, even if they seek the worst for us."[4]

Love means a momma gets up at the cry of her child in need even if it's 3:30 A.M., not because of a feeling but because of commitment. She has made the decision to love her child.

SpiritFruit love is one of God's gifts to us made real by the Holy Spirit. This love is intended to be passed on in our relationships to others. It's basic to all of the other graces of the Spirit.

Remember, love is of divine origin. So the best way to understand it is to see how our God displays it. Look at John 3:16. "For God so loved the world, that he gave his one and only Son, that whoever believes in him shall not perish but have eternal life." That's a definition of love! Stuart Briscoe says, "Agape moved down to earth in mighty force and agape lifts earth to heaven in transforming power. Agape sent God to man and ever since has raised man to God."[5]

Throughout eternity, God loved. Through the winding roads of Old Testament sin and failure, God still loved. In Jeremiah 31:3 God says, "The LORD appeared to us in the past, saying: 'I have loved you with an everlasting love; I have drawn you with loving-kindness.'" How's that description of love? Everlasting. The Hebrew carries the idea "from vanishing point to vanishing point." That means God was love as far as you can see in eternity past and God will still be love as far as you can see into eternity future. The kids today might say, "God's love is way cool!"

In the New Testament, love is shown through the gift of God's Son, Jesus Christ. We witness the life of Jesus from his birth to his death. Jesus displayed love every day, in every way, all the way. Finally, love brought Jesus to the cross. Paul describes it like this, "But God demonstrates his own love for us in this: While we were still sinners, Christ died for us" (Rom. 5:8). At the cross God proved his love for the world in the death of his Son Jesus.

A selfish boy pressures his girlfriend to compromise her purity: "If you love me, prove it." What he is really saying is, "Satisfy me." No love there!

In John 13:1, the Bible says ". . . having loved his own who were in the world, he now showed them the full extent of his love." The phrase could be translated literally, "He loved them all the way." Jesus loved us all the way! Have you ever thought that Jesus could have quit loving at any place throughout his life? He loved people, healing them and helping them. He received very little in return. Jesus could have said, "If that's the way they are, I'm out of here! I'm going back to heaven." But he didn't. He kept on going—denying himself and serving others. He went all the way. One day he bore a cross up a hill called Calvary, laid himself on it, spread his arms and said, "I love you this much." This is the great proof and pattern of divine love.

Remember playing with daisies as a kid? You had a crush on Mable Whisenhant at school, didn't you? So you pulled the little petals from the daisies saying, "She loves me; she loves me not; she loves me; she loves me not." The last one always was, "She loves me." True confession: I rigged it, didn't you? At the cross, every drop of blood that fell from the body of our Lord said, "I love you; I love you; I love you." Galatians 2:20 puts it this way, ". . . who loved me, and gave himself for me." No wonder the hymn writer said, "When I survey the wondrous cross. . . . Did ere such love and sorrow meet?"

C. S. Lewis says, "God, who needs nothing, loves into existence superfluous creatures in order that he may love and perfect them . . ."[6]

Christ's love for us should be the pattern we use to love others. Ephesians 5:2 (KJV) says, "And walk in love, as Christ also hath loved us. . . ." The Holy Spirit in our hearts is able to produce this love in our relationships with others.

Love Described

Love is vertical, meaning it deals with our love for God above. This is seen in many places in the Bible (see Rom. 8:28; 2 Thess. 3:5). But love is also horizontal, referring to our love for other people. I believe this is the primary emphasis of SpiritFruit love. Paul talks about the graces of the Spirit that characterize our relationships with others. Timothy George says, "The result of the transforming, sanctifying ministry of the Holy Spirit in our lives is just this: that we are enabled to love one another with the same kind of love that God loves us."[7] Think about it. Jesus often emphasizes, "Love one another," doesn't he?

First Corinthians 13 is "de bomb" when it comes to love in the Bible. In this chapter, love for others is wrapped up in plain, easy-to-understand packages. A. T. Robertson describes this chapter as a sweet bell between the jangling noise of 1 Corinthians 12 and 14. Remember the importance of context in studying Scripture. You've heard the phrase "Location, location, location!" Apply that to your Bible study and consider all Scripture in its correct context.

The Corinthian believers were enamored with the gifts. According to 1 Corinthians 1:7, all the gifts were present in the Corinthian church, but the Corinthian Christians were lacking in the love department! They were so intrigued with the gifts that they neglected the graces of the Spirit. First Corinthians 12 ends by saying, "But eagerly desire the greater gifts" (v. 31). Then 1 Corinthians 14 says, "Follow the way of love and eagerly desire spiritual gifts, especially the gift of prophecy" (v. 1). Right in the middle of this discussion of the gifts of the Spirit is a detailed description of how love operates in relationships. This is how it works! Let's untie and unpack these love packages and look at their contents.

Love is patient. Literally it means "fire stretched out." Peterson paraphrases: "Love never gives up" (*The Message*). This means love has a long fuse. Christians filled with the SpiritFruit of love don't blow up when the waitress at the restaurant forgets the French fries.

Love is kind. This means being a calm person. Peterson renders it, "Love cares more for others than for itself." The Spirit-filled believer who is living in love allows someone with a few items to go ahead of him or her at the grocery store check-out.

It does not envy. Love is not jealous. Peterson says, "Love doesn't want what it doesn't have." When love is flowing in your life, you are not upset when someone else at work receives the promotion you wanted. The success of others doesn't produce jealousy. Vance Havner used to say, "Christians are like matches—they strike only on their own boxes."

It does not boast. That is, love marches in no parade. It doesn't show off. Peterson says, "Love doesn't strut." The Christian living in love does not have to be noticed. People admire the peacock because of the grandeur of its plumes until they are driven off by the squawking voice! Christians don't have to honk their own horn.

It is not proud. Peterson's take is love "doesn't have a swelled head." Think personal economy. Pride is the hardest kind of runaway inflation to check, isn't it?

It is not rude. Peterson says love "doesn't force itself on others." This means love has good manners. Christians who are filled with SpiritFruit love are polite, not rude and crude. They don't interrupt the conversations of others. They are courteous in their dealings with all people.

It is not self-seeking. Peterson paraphrases, love "isn't always 'me first.'" The Spirit-filled believer doesn't have to be first in everything. If Spirit-love is flowing in your life, you don't get upset if you aren't the first in the Wednesday night supper line, or if you don't get the first parking space in the lot at Dillard's.

It is not easily angered. In other words, love is not easily irritated. Peterson puts it this way, love "doesn't fly off the handle." When you live in the atmosphere of Holy Spirit love, you don't blow up or lose your cool when someone says something unpleasant to you.

It keeps no record of wrongs. This means love doesn't count. Peterson says love "doesn't keep score of the sins of others." If you are letting love be produced in your life, you are willing to forgive your mate when he or she has acted in a hateful way. You keep no records. One guy said, "Every time my wife and I have a fuss, she gets *historical*." His friend said, "You mean *hysterical?*" "No," he said, "*historical*. She brings up every thing I've ever done wrong."

Love does not delight in evil, but rejoices with the truth. I like how Peterson puts it: love "doesn't revel when others grovel." When you live in love, you want to hear good news about people instead of bad news. Gossip? Does a juicy little piece of news get you going? Then you are rejoicing in the report of sin.

It always protects. This means to cover or protect. Peterson says, love "puts up with anything." When you are filled with Spirit-love, you don't drag the faults of other people into the light.

Always protects, always perseveres. Love believes the best about people.

Always hopes. Love is always optimistic.

Always perseveres. It endures all things. It never gives up on people.

Are these traits in your life? Do they characterize how you relate to other people? This is the best way to tell if you are a Spirit-filled Christian. Not the flashy gifts but this beautiful grace, this sweet fruit of the Spirit—love.

Love Desired

Drescher tells of a little girl who was frightened by the thunder of an approaching storm one night. Her father held her as he explained that there was no need to fear since God would take care of her because he loved her. The little girl said, "I know God will take care of me and loves me, but right now, Daddy, I want someone with skin on to love me."[8]

Christians, we are to be God's love with skin on. It is fine to explain and even to define love. Yet we must express love in our relationships with others. This is where it's at!

Have you ever noticed how often love is connected with giving in the Bible? John 3:16, "For God so loved . . . that he gave." Ephesians 5:25, "Husbands, love your wives, just as Christ loved the church and gave himself up for her." Galatians 2:20, ". . . God, who loved me and gave himself for me."

Love always gives. Love moves toward the need for love in the hearts of others. People need love; they desire love. Therefore, love is not just an emotion for us to experience—love is an action we take to meet the desire for love in the hearts of people. Remember, love is a noun and an action verb!

First Thessalonians 3:12 gives an interesting insight about this Spirit-love. "May the Lord make your love increase and overflow for each other and for everyone else, just as ours does for you." Love can be an expanding, growing thing. We also learn that love is desired and needed in our relationships with two other groups of people.

Love for Other Believers

Spirit-love needs to be expressed to saints. Christians need our love. First Peter 1:22 says, ". . . love one another deeply, from the heart." What about those saints closest to you, those who live at your house? The members of your family desire to be loved. The family should be a place where love lives and increases.

Two boys in Vietnam were hunkered down in a ditch. Bombs were bursting, bullets were whistling, and grenades were exploding all around them. "Isn't this awful?" said one of the boys. "Not really," the other boy said, "it just reminds me of home." Sad, but too often true. Without love, home becomes a war zone. It becomes just a place where people sleep at night, park their car, watch TV, catch a bowl of cereal, or grab a shower.

Do you love your family? Ever say it? Show it? First Peter 3:8ff. gives some helpful ways to show us how love can come alive in our family. "Finally, all of you, live in harmony with one another." What does it mean to "live in harmony with one another"? It means talking to each other. Do you talk to your family members? Do you ever tell them that you love them? Every day you should express your love to every member of your family. "Be sympathetic." This probably means we need sympathy for one another's stresses and problems. When family members come in at the end of the work day, they bring all kinds of problems and difficulties. Are you sympathetic? Dad had a hard day on the job. Do you express concern for his frustration? Sue encountered a real problem with a teacher at school. Do you enter into her hurt? Mom got an upsetting call from a friend. Do you share in her anxiety?

"Love as brothers, be compassionate and humble." We should treat one another with respect. I've always wondered why some families seem more courteous to strangers who enter their home than to the people who live there. We should treat one another with kindness. "Be compassionate." That means we are to be kind to each other in the family. "Be humble." Are you kind and courteous in public, then rude and selfish at home? *That your prayers be not hindered*. Spiritual life is affected when love is lacking in the family. Family prayer means little if it is not supported and surrounded by Spirit-love.

Do you love your family? Of course you do. Lost people and Christians alike love their mates and children. Yet, think about it. The highest degree of love is possible only when the Holy Spirit pours his love into our hearts and produces love through us.

The members of our church family also need and desire love. I think about Paul's interesting statement in Colossians 1:4, "Because we have heard of your faith in Christ Jesus and of the love you have for all the saints." All the saints. Not just the sweet saints—the sour ones also. Not just the happy saints—the unhappy ones too. I heard a little poem a few years ago I like to use:

"To dwell above with saints we love,

that will indeed be glory.

To live below with saints we know;

well, that's another story!"

Ever thought about how the disciples reacted the night Jesus said, "By this all men will know that you are my disciples, if you love one another" (John 13:35)? I can imagine John cutting his eyes toward Peter and thinking, *Is he saying I have to love that loud-mouthed Peter?* Or I see Peter cut his eyes at Thomas and think, *Have I got to love that pessimistic, doubting Thomas?* But that's exactly what Jesus meant. We must show love in our relationships with our fellow believers.

Like the family, the church is to be an orchard where we cultivate the grace of love for one another. First John 4:20 specifically says, "If anyone says, 'I love God,' yet hates his brother, he is a liar. For anyone who does not love his brother, whom he has seen, cannot love God, whom he has not seen." Only the Holy Spirit can help us love the way we ought to love.

Where love is lacking, a church's worship is affected. Even with all the gifts operating, worship without love produces disruption, competition, and pride. A church's work is affected, too. Did you know you can labor and not love, but you cannot love and not labor? First Thessalonians 1:3 uses the phrase *labor prompted by love*. Too many Christians labor in the church but aren't motivated by love. The Ephesian church had this problem. Jesus wrote them a second New Testament letter in which he praised them for their works and labor (Rev. 2:2–3). So, what was the problem? They had left their first love (Rev. 2:4). They were working and laboring, but it was all a boring chore. SpiritFruit love was not motivating what they did.

Without love, a church's witness is hindered. Sinners need the love which we can express. Yes, we learn to love saints in the church, but we also learn to love sinners. There is a desire in the human heart to be loved. Think about it. As a society we constantly grow farther and farther apart. We don't meet at neighborhood stores—we go to twenty-four hour super-stores. Instead of talking with our neighbors over the back fence, we communicate silently and anonymously over the Internet. Are we really just so many credit cards, E-mail addresses, and answering machines? You know what? People are suffering from isolation, loneliness, and feelings of insignificance.

Ron Hembree shares a sad story. A young father shot himself in a bar phone booth. A child's folded crayon drawing was found in his pocket. He had written on the paper, "Please leave in my coat pocket. I want to have it buried with me." In the note the man told the sad story of his daughter, Shirley Lee, who had perished in a fire five months before. The father was so grief-stricken at her death he asked total strangers to attend so she would have a nice service. There were no other family members. Her mother had been dead since the little girl was two. The father couldn't stand the loneliness or the loss, so he took his life.[9] People are dying for love.

Love for the Lost

Some people are easy to love. Others aren't. How big is the circle of your love? All around you are lonely, loveless people. People are crying out from all directions, "Notice me." No, they don't say it with words, but they say it by bizarre dress and extreme behavior. They do it by earrings and tattoos, phony smiles and plastic "hellos." They are trying to cope with their loneliness with a bottle or a needle or a pill.

Do you see the lonely people? They walk by you every day in your office. You see them on park benches. You observe them withdrawing on school playgrounds. They even sit in the corners of our church auditoriums. Too often we fail to see the loneliness, hurt, and sorrow people carry on the inside.

Jesus loved people. He was "moved with compassion" when he saw people. SpiritFruit love is the kind of love Jesus showed people. If we let this kind of love flow through us, it will change our lives, causing us to seek opportunities to love others. Talk to a lonely old person. *Agape* love makes us sincerely take interest in others instead of being wrapped up in and focused on the tiny details of our lives.

Remember, love is a decision, a choice. You must decide to love unlovely people. It's a matter of will. When that teen cuts you off—the one in front of you in traffic, radio blaring obscene music—you choose to love him. When the neighbor lets his dog tear up your flower garden, you decide to love her.

I heard of this wealthy lady who was visiting a low-rent childcare center with a social worker. A little girl, dirty and shabby, nudged up against the wealthy lady. The lady pulled away and said, "Why doesn't her mother bathe her?" The social worker quietly replied, "Her mother loves the child but doesn't hate dirt. It's obvious you hate dirt. Do you love the child?"

Remember Zacchaeus? A crooked money-grabber. How did Jesus win him? He just loved him. How did Jesus win the immoral, smart-mouthed woman at the well? He just loved her. It's the only way to reach people and win them for the Lord. It works!

Pittsburgh built a large, modern post office some years ago. On dedication day a large crowd attended and high school bands played. The time came to send the first letter. Much to the chagrin of the engineers and architects, there was no slot anywhere in the building![10] Might be nice on tax day! You know what? Love is the slot. If love is missing, the message of Jesus can't be sent out and delivered.

We can't love the lost or anybody else unless we allow the Holy Spirit to produce his love in and through us. When I was a boy I remember singing this song, "Lord, lay some soul upon my heart and love that soul through me." We are commanded to love. Over and over again the New Testament admonishes *love*. We should try to obey the commandment.

Often, we are unable to love as we should. This drives us to our knees in prayer. We confess to the Lord how unlovely we are in our relationships with others. We ask the Lord to help us love. We yield to the control of the Holy Spirit. As we do, we find ourselves growing in the fruit of love for others. And as Philippians 1:9 says: "that your love may abound more and more in knowledge and depth of insight."

"What's love got to do with it?" Tina Turner asks. Everything! Love is the first fruit plucked in the harvest of the Christ-life. It is the first fruit produced in a Spirit-filled life. Love sets the standard. It is the measuring stick. It provides the motive and the impetus for the joy and the peace and the patience and all the other graces to follow. Love is the foundation to all the other fruits because, really, all the other fruits are various forms of love. Think about that!

CHAPTER 4

JUST PEACHY!

Picture this! I'm ten, OK? It's a hot, hot August day. I'm really thirsty and I'm standing in front of a peach tree. Push PAUSE!!!

Oh, the peach . . . the epitome of summer fruit. Why? Because a peach has a high water content and just a few calories. The smooth, sweet flavor is quite refreshing. Bet you didn't know that the peach is the third-most-popular fruit in America, right behind the apple and the orange? Peaches just go with everything from ice cream to pound cake. Don't you think?

Now push PLAY! OK, you can use your remote control! Back to the hot, hot day . . . Yeah, yeah, yeah. OK, I pluck a big, soft, fuzzy peach from the tree. I take a thirsty bite. Whoa! An explosion of flavor, almost like that slogan for Skittles candy, "Taste the rainbow."

Spanish colonizers planted peach trees in California. Early explorers and settlers planted them up and down the eastern seaboard. There are many varieties of peaches—two are the Elberta and the Belle of Georgia. (Being from Georgia, the Peach State, I especially like that one!) A peach is very close to a nectarine. A single gene causes the peach to be fuzzy, whereas the lack of that gene causes the nectarine to be smooth skinned. The peach is the prima donna among fruit trees.

Because it is an early bloomer, it is extra sensitive to cold weather. Peaches provide many health benefits. They are easily digested. They stimulate the digestive juices, improve the health of the skin, and add color to one's complexion.[1]

The peach juice is thick and syrupy as it runs down my chin on the outside and down my throat on the inside. Peach juice is all over me—on my chin, on my chest, and on my hands and arms. It's even dripping down to my bare toes! I have the peach, peach, peach (just like the "joy, joy, joy" from that old Vacation Bible School song) all over me, and I feel the joy and it's *just peachy!*

What is the joy or this peachy feeling all about? It's one of the themes of the Bible. The words *joy* and *joyful* occur approximately 250 times. The verb form *rejoice* occurs about 200 times. Gives you the idea God is interested in our joy, doesn't it?

The Old Testament is filled with joy. We often think of the Old Testament as a book of blood and judgment. All that war, pain, and sorrow make a pretty sad book, right? Well, the sadness is certainly there. But there is also a strong note of joy. Kaufman Kohler says there is no language with as many words for *joy* as the Hebrew. He says that in the Old Testament there are thirteen Hebrew roots and twenty-seven words that convey the idea of joy.[2] What are these words? Briscoe points out several. One is *simchah*. It means "bright and shining," like the bright eyes of a two-year-old on Christmas morning. Or like a bride coming down the aisle on her wedding day. A second word is *masos*. This word means "leaping or jumping." Think of the crippled man at the gate leaping and jumping after he was healed. A third word is *rinnah*, meaning "shouting, an exuberant expression of joy." A fourth word, *gil*, means "moving around in a circle."[3] Studying the Old Testament helps us mean it when we sing, "I've got the joy, joy, joy, joy."

In the New Testament, by contrast, the primary word for joy is *chara*. It occurs about sixty times. *Rejoice* occurs seventy-two. What's up with New Testament joy? Barclay helps us define it. He says that it "most often describes that joy which has a basis in religion and whose foundation is God." He continues, "It is not the joy that comes from earthly things or cheap thrills."[4] You want more about the word? Well, the Greek root for joy is the same as the word for grace. Joy is *chara*, grace is *charis*. Grace is the basis of God's favor toward us that produces joy. Because we can know God's grace, we can experience his joy. So when we read that the fruit of the Spirit is joy, we celebrate what God has done for us. Peterson paraphrases joy as "an exuberance about life."

Joy and happiness. What's the difference? Happiness depends upon what happens. We are happy when what happens to us is pleasant. It's the "Zippety doo dah, zippety dee day . . . everything's going my way" kind of experience. But joy is different. Joy does not depend on external circumstances. Joy is not a fair-weather feeling. It is fruit produced by the Holy Spirit in the believer's life. Remember that the fruit of the Spirit is love, then joy. So joy is connected to love. We cannot know God's joy until we know God's love. Drescher says, "Joy is love smiling."

Think about it. Since joy is produced by the Holy Spirit, we know it is divine. The Heavenly Father is the source of joy. "Rejoice in the Lord!" (Phil. 3:1). "Rejoice in the Lord always" (Phil. 4:4). "Rejoice in God" (Rom. 5:11). Psalm 16:11 says, "You have made known to me the path of life; / you will fill me with joy in your presence, / with eternal pleasures at your right hand."

The Son of God, Jesus, is also the source of joy. He is the perfect picture of joy. Everything about his coming into the world was accompanied with joy. Great joy resulted when his birth was announced (Luke 1:28). The shepherds were told of a joyful coming of the Savior (Luke 2:10). The wise men had great joy at the arrival of the Messiah (Matt. 2:10). Think about his life on earth. As Jesus ministered, he brought joy to people by healing their sicknesses (Luke 13:17). Even in his death, there was joy (Heb. 12:2). When the Lord Jesus was raised from the dead, joy filled his followers (Matt. 28:8). As he ascended back to heaven, the disciples felt great joy (Luke 24:52; John 14:28). See, Jesus actually left joy for us as a benefit of his will (John 15:11).

Divine Holy Spirit joy is much deeper than fun or fluffy feel-goods. It is not just an add-on to our lives. Like fruit, Holy Spirit joy comes from the life within. Drescher quotes Principal Rainy, who said, "Joy is the flag which is flown from the castle of the heart when the king is in residence there."[5] The divine grace of joy is produced in and through the life of a believer by the Holy Spirit. Note that Romans 14:17 talks about joy *in the Holy Spirit*. First Thessalonians 1:6 refers to the joy *given by the Holy Spirit*. Joy is, therefore, a divine grace produced in and through the lives of believers as they yield to the Holy Spirit. Let's consider SpiritFruit joy and see just how peachy it is.

Possible

SpiritFruit joy is made possible by knowing the Lord. Briscoe says, "Joy comes from rightly understanding and appreciating theological truth."[6] Our understanding about the truth of salvation is designed to bring joy to our lives. Romans 15:13 says, "May the God of hope fill you with all joy and peace as you trust in him, so that you may overflow with hope by the power of the Holy Spirit."

The salvation experience brings joy. I have always been glad that Jesus describes salvation in joyful terms. Remember his parable about the great supper in Luke 14? Jesus describes his salvation as a feast, not a funeral. Too many Christians convey the idea that coming to Christ removes all joy. The devil has convinced many that giving their lives to Christ would take away their joy. Hey, some Christians don't help much. Too many go around with a tombstone under one arm and a coffin under the other. But Jesus indicates that salvation is a happy time like a wedding, not a somber time like a burial.

Let's think about this salvation joy. Remember the Ethiopian eunuch? When Philip led him to Christ, he "went on his way rejoicing" (Acts 8:39). Jesus told his disciples something interesting. They had been sent out to cast out demons. They came back rejoicing that they were able to do so. But Jesus said, ". . . do not rejoice that the spirits submit to you, but rejoice that your names are written in heaven" (Luke 10:20). Why did Jesus say that? Because he knew they might not always be successful in casting out demons. (Check out when Jesus came down from the Mount of Transfiguration in Matthew 17.) But their names were to be a perpetual, eternal source of joy in heaven.

When you think about all that goes with your salvation, you can't help but feel joy. Salvation means your sins are forgiven! You are a member of God's family! You are going to heaven when you die! You have the personal presence of the Lord in your life! There's a purpose and plan for your life! The result? You feel "just peachy!" God owns you.

Think about hope. Salvation brings us joy because it produces hope in our lives. Romans 5:2 says, ". . . rejoice in the hope of the glory of God." First Peter 1:8 says, "Though you have not seen him, you love him; and even though you do not see him now, you believe in him and are filled with an inexpressible and glorious joy."

Ever consider your future? The joy of salvation does have a future dimension. We will see our loved ones again. We will see Jesus again. We will receive rewards for faithfulness to Jesus. This equals great joy in our lives.

As I understand the Bible, our salvation cannot be lost. But we can lose our joy. Remember the dark page in the life of David? He was a man after God's own heart, truly a saved man, yet adultery put a black smudge on his life. When he confessed his sin to the Lord he said, "Restore to me the joy of your salvation" (Ps. 51:12). He didn't say restore *salvation*. He said restore the *joy* of it. Sin and joy can't live in the same heart. Picture sin as a vacuum cleaner sucking the joy out of the human heart.

SpiritFruit joy is produced by living for the Lord. Paul says, ". . . nor to put their hope in wealth, which is so uncertain, but to put their hope in God, who richly provides us with everything for our enjoyment" (1 Tim. 6:17). Think about it. God has given us everything for our joy! Look around you. The birds, the rocks, the flowers, and the trees. All are there for our joy. Friends and books, coffee and cheesecake. All are things to enjoy. Knowing Christ and having the fullness of the Spirit bring joy to our lives.

Those who don't know our Lord may think the Christian life is not "way cool." As I have mentioned, some Christians don't help much. Talking about the cross, the blood, and sin and judgment doesn't sound too "with it." Yet, properly understood, living for the Lord means living life filled with joy.

I read about a Christian missionary who was flying home from an over-seas assignment after the Korean War. A group of GIs were on her plane. They were partying—beer all over the cabin, cigarettes lit up. The soldiers offered her a drink or a cigarette many times. Each time she answered, "No, thank you, I don't need it." After a while one of the GIs said to her, "Every time we ask you to have a drink or a smoke, you say, 'No, I don't need it.' Why do you keep saying that?" She responded, "I'll be glad to tell you why. You are seeking joy. I already have joy on the inside. There was a time when I came to the end of my rope. I found Jesus, the giver of real joy, at the end of my rope. I don't need these other things."[7] Unfortunately, some people (maybe even these GIs) think Jesus makes you sad rather than glad. People think God looks down from heaven searching to find one of his children enjoying himself. When he finds one, he shouts, "Stop it!!" Not so. Joy is living a high-end life.

Living for the Lord produces internal joy. But this internal joy is expressed on the outside. How can you tell? One way is by praise. James asks, "Is any [among you] merry? let him sing psalms" (James 5:13). Someone said that joy is the pressure in the system, and praise is the safety valve letting it go. In our attempts to express emotionalism, let's not stifle Holy Spirit joy.

Joy also comes by serving the Lord. Christians testify that they experience joy in service for Jesus Christ. Think about the apostle Paul. After his Damascus Road experience he spent the rest of his life doing what Jesus wanted him to do. As he came to the end of the road, he had a great desire in his heart. He said, "However, I consider my life worth nothing to me, if only I may finish the race and complete the task the Lord Jesus has given me" (Acts 20:24a).

The Lord brings joy in our lives in many ways, but the greatest joy a Christian can experience comes in leading another person to Christ. Paul indicates this in Philippians 4:1: "Therefore, my brothers, you whom I love and long for, my joy and crown, that is how you should stand firm in the Lord, dear friends!" And in his statements in 1 Thessalonians 2:19–20: "For what is our hope, our joy, or the crown in which we will glory in the presence of our Lord Jesus when he comes? Is it not you? Indeed, you are our glory and joy."

Every person who has led someone else to Christ knows this joy. Psalm 126:5 says, "Those who sow in tears / will reap with songs of joy." The next verse, 126:6, is my life verse. Picture a farmer coming out of the harvest field with a bundle of sheathes on his shoulder. Some render the verse, *with songs of joy*. One of the happiest scenes in our First Baptist Church, Jacksonville, is invitation time when members of our church bring forward people whom they have personally led to Christ. It's joy, joy, joy everywhere, and it's just peachy.

Did you ever have to give a report in school? Nervous, huh! Well, one day we will give our final report to Jesus. As a pastor, I have spent many years serving the Lord Jesus and seeking to lead others to know him as Savior. I can say that I look forward to the time when I can report to the Lord about my joy in serving him as a pastor (see Heb. 13:17). Imagine the joy in hearing Jesus say, "Well done, good and faithful servant! You have been faithful with a few things; I will put you in charge of many things. Come and share your master's happiness!" (Matt. 25:21). Now that sounds peachy!

Incredible

When considering this SpiritFruit joy, you may see a paradox. Joy is found where it is least expected. As one who grew up in a small town, I know that joy has some unusual connections. Happiness and difficult circumstances don't jive. Happiness and unhappiness can't go together. But, joy and affliction can (2 Thess. 1:6). Joy and sorrow can (2 Cor. 6:10). What's up with that? Well, joy is independent of circumstances. It's out there! No experience in life can destroy this divine, supernatural SpiritFruit joy. You want to own this joy? Read on!

Even when we suffer, we can experience joy. Paul talked about this to the Colossian believers. He said, "I rejoice in what was suffered for you" (Col. 1:24). The Christian rejoices in his suffering. Huh? Well, read Romans 5:4-5: "Perseverance, character; and character, hope. And hope does not disappoint us, because God has poured out his love into our hearts by the Holy Spirit, whom he has given us." Say what? Don't forget verse 3. You see that word *know?* The Christian rejoices in suffering because he knows it is part of the maturing process. This is not about some sadistic enjoyment of suffering. It's about God using everything in our lives to make us like Jesus. The thought of being like Jesus is what brings us joy.

Read James 1:2. James talks about all kinds of hard times and he says, *Consider it pure joy.* Total joy is what he means. The KJV says, "Count it all joy." What's the deal? Don't leave out verse 3. "Knowing this, that the trying of your faith worketh patience" (James 1:3 KJV). There it is again—the word *knowing.* Joy is around because Christians know that the different trials in life produce patience. The joy is in knowing what's coming. Instead of saying, "Yeah, right" the next time you see a Christian experiencing joy during a trial, you could say, "That's just peachy!"

You probably know that Philippians has been called the joy book of the New Testament. Paul talks about joy and rejoicing almost twenty times. "It's easy for him to talk about joy," you say. "He's swinging in a hammock at the pool deck of the Corinthian Hilton. Pretty girls are bringing him tropical fruit smoothies. He's chillin'! Easy for him to talk about joy." Well, not really. When Paul wrote the joy book, he was incarcerated in a Roman jail. Any day might be his last. Yet all the way through we hear him singing,

"I've got the joy, joy, joy, joy down in my heart." Or he might be saying, "I'm just peachy!"

Cyprian, bishop of Carthage, wrote a friend in the third century:

This seems to be a cheerful world, Donatus, when I view it from this fair garden under the shadow of these vines. But if I climb some great mountain and look out over the wide lands, you know very well what I see—brigands on the road, pirates on the seas; in the amphitheaters people murdering each other to please the applauding crowds and under all roofs I see misery and self-ishness. It is really a bad world, Donatus, an incredibly bad world.

Yet in the midst of it, I have found a quiet and holy people. They have discovered the joy which is a thousand times better than any pleasure of the sinful life. They are despised and perse-cuted, but they care not. These people, Donatus, are Christians and I am one of them.[8]

Christians experience this supernatural joy even in times of suffering. There is something about this joy which has roots in the cross of Calvary. This grounds a Christian's joy, no matter what the circumstances.

Joy can be experienced even in persecution. Remember that novel, *A Tale of Two Cities*, by Charles Dickens? His first line read, "It was the best of times, it was the worst of times." Well, a Christian possesses joy in both the best and worst times. Jesus taught that his joy would be independent of whatever adversities Christians might face. He said, "Blessed are those who are persecuted because of righteousness, for theirs is the kingdom of heaven. Blessed are you when people insult you, persecute you and falsely say all kinds of evil against you because of me. Rejoice and be glad, because great is your reward in heaven, for in the same way they persecuted the prophets who were before you" (Matt. 5:10–12).

You know suffering? The apostles surely did! Read about their persecu-tion in Acts 5. Then, read in amazement verses 40–41: "His speech per-suaded them. They called the apostles in and had them flogged. Then they ordered them not to speak in the name of Jesus, and let them go. The apos-tles left the Sanhedrin, rejoicing because they had been counted worthy of suffering disgrace for the Name." Or see what they experienced in Acts 13.

Then check out verses 50–52: "But the Jews incited the God-fearing women of high standing and the leading men of the city. They stirred up persecution against Paul and Barnabas, and expelled them from their region. So they shook the dust from their feet in protest against them and went to Iconium. And the disciples were filled with joy and with the Holy Spirit."

Alexander Maclaren says, "Joy may grow in the very face of danger as a slender rose bush flings its bright sprays and fragrant flowers over the top of a cataract."[9] In the midst of trouble, this otherworldly joy of the Lord becomes a supernatural source of strength. Maybe *The X Files* will do an episode on the unexplainable phenomenon of Christian joy. Not likely! Nehemiah 8:10 says, ". . . For the joy of the LORD is your strength." Here is joy so deep, no evil act, unkindness of others, or negative circumstance can penetrate it.

This SpiritFruit joy can also be known in death. The death of a loved one is an overwhelming experience. Christians grieve over the loss of loved ones just like everyone else. The burden and sorrow can be impossible to bear. The day is dark. The hurt is heavy. In the midst of it, Christians seek God's help. The Holy Spirit pours out supernatural joy. This is "joy in the Holy Spirit!" Even when facing one's own death this joy can be and is present.

Picture a late night. Jesus is meeting for the last time with his disciples. He will be crucified at nine o'clock the next morning. Jesus says, "I have told you this so that my joy may be in you and that your joy may be complete" (John 15:11). "I tell you the truth, you will weep and mourn while the world rejoices. You will grieve, but your grief will turn to joy" (John 16:20). ". . . but when her baby is born she forgets the anguish because of her joy that a child is born into the world" (v. 21). "So with you: Now is your time of grief, but I will see you again and you will rejoice, and no one will take away your joy" (John v. 22). "Until now you have not asked for anything in my name. Ask and you will receive, and your joy will be complete" (John v. 24). "I am coming to you now, but I say these things while I am still in the world, so that they may have the full measure of my joy within them" (John 17:13).

His joy! Hebrews 12:2 says, "Let us fix our eyes on Jesus, the author and perfecter of our faith, who for the joy set before him endured the cross, scorning its shame, and sat down at the right hand of the throne of God." How could Jesus face his death on the cross with joy? Because he knew there was meaning to his death. The joy of multitudes and multitudes of people being saved filled his heart during his death.

Paul also experienced joy as he faced death. I have been in the prison where it is believed Paul lived his last days. From here he wrote his last letter to young Timothy. As one reads 2 Timothy there is a sense of joy and anticipation as Paul awaits his death. Holy Spirit joy can leap over prison walls. Holy Spirit joy can carry us through even the lonely time of death.

Archaeologists once uncovered a letter written by a soon-to-be Christian martyr. Just before death the martyr wrote, "In a dark hole I have found cheerfulness; in a place of bitterness and death I have found rest. Who would believe that in a state of misery I have had great pleasure; that in a lonely corner I have had glorious company, and in the hardest bonds perfect repose? All these things Jesus has granted me. He is with me, comforts me, and fills me with joy. He drives bitterness from me and fills me with strength and consolation."[10] From that martyr's day until this twenty-first century, Christians have experienced and still experience supernatural joy when they meet death. It may sound trite, but a Christian can keep his or her "just peachy" joy even when facing death.

Transferable

Remember, fruit is not produced to benefit the tree. SpiritFruit is produced on trees too. The trees I'm referring to are you and me, the Christians seeking to yield to the Holy Spirit. Obviously, we know that SpiritFruit joy does bless us and help us. But, it's not only for our benefit. We must share the joy with those around us. SpiritFruit joy is to be a blessing to those all around us.

There is something contagious about the Christian who shows SpiritFruit joy. Drescher says, "Joy is the seasoning that tickles the taste buds of the unsaved." Joy can be compared to a well filled with sweet water.

The water is not useful unless it is brought to the surface. Far too many Christians do not let the joy of the Lord surface in their lives.[11]

To be most effective in witnessing, the Lord Jesus and his gospel should be displayed in all their joyfulness. Jesus showed joy in his earthly ministry. We have no record in the Gospels that Jesus laughed. But think about it. Don't you think he did? Though he was a man of sorrow, he talked too much about joy never to have smiled. How about this comment? "Did Jesus ever laugh?" "I don't know, but he certainly fixed me up so I can laugh."[12]

Little children were drawn to Jesus. Do you know any children drawn to a drab, dull, dismal person? There must have been such a joy and exuberance about Jesus that little children liked to be around him. Sinners usually don't invite dead heads to their parties. Yet Jesus was known as *a friend of sinners*. He actually was invited to their parties. Do sinners want you to be around? Do you think they would have wanted Jesus around if he'd been a geek? They certainly wouldn't have invited a killjoy to dinner. No. I believe Jesus showed joy all over.

There are indications that the New Testament Christians had such joy that people were drawn to them. This indicates to me the early Christians had a joy that was catching. "Praising God, and enjoying the favor of all the people" (Acts 2:47). I believe Christians today have a responsibility to demonstrate and transfer the joy of the Lord.

Our joy should be transferred to others. The gospel shouts out joy, doesn't it? There is joy in telling about it. Jesus said, "Even now the reaper draws his wages, even now he harvests the crop for eternal life, so that the sower and the reaper may be glad together" (John 4:36). When joy is shared, heaven is filled with it, "and goes home. Then he calls his friends and neighbors together and says, 'Rejoice with me; I have found my lost sheep.' I tell you that in the same way there will be more rejoicing in heaven over one sinner who repents than over ninety-nine righteous persons who do not need to repent" (Luke 15:6–7). When believers hear about others coming to Christ through the gospel message, joy is produced. "The church sent them on their way, and as they traveled through Phoenicia and Samaria, they told how the Gentiles had been converted. This news made all the brothers very glad" (Acts 15:3). (See also Acts 8:8; 13:48; Phil. 1:18.)

We share our message of joy and that brings joy to people. See 2 Corinthians 1:24 and Philippians 1:25. Too many people have the idea that giving the gospel to people means removing the joy from it. I agree that the initial truths of the gospel may make us squirm. It is not joyful to hear that we are sinners in danger of eternal death (see Rom. 3:23; 6:23). But when one hears the good news that Jesus died, was buried, and rose again to cover our sins and to conquer them, the human heart should perk up a bit. Then, we invite Jesus into our hearts, and all the joy that salvation brings comes pouring in. Then we can sing, "We have heard the joyful sound, / Jesus saves, Jesus saves."

The gospel miracle should be transferred. Because we have experienced this miracle of salvation, we should bring all of this joy to others. The most joyful, happy, attractive people in a city or town should be its Christians.

I know joy is not just a silly grin. But I do believe the joy of the Lord should help us at least look pleasant. Psalm 90:17 says, "May the favor of the Lord our God rest upon us." When Moses came down from the mountain, having been in the presence of God, his face was shining. If we are to draw people to Jesus, radiance and attractiveness about our lives should be reflected on our faces. Holy exuberance is certainly part of the package that attracts others to us and to Christ.

Do you know Nietzsche? He was a miserable atheist. To read his writings is a miserable experience! But listen to what he said to some Christians: "You are going to have to look more redeemed than you do if we are to believe the message of redemption."[13] If we are full of the Holy Spirit, we should radiate the fullness of joy to those we meet. Hey, I know people are different. Different people express their emotions in different ways, don't they? But can't we agree that there should be some basic expression of joyfulness in the life and on the face of a Christian? Let's try to look peachy!

This is probably one of the biggies. Christians may fail to be effective in their outreach because they lack joy. When the prodigal son came home, which appealed to him more? The scowl of his older brother? Or the smile of his father? You know the answer.

We should live lives that bring the joy of the Lord to others. See, I want to be a source of joy to my wife, Janet. I want to bring joy to my children.

I want other Christians around me to experience joy because of their contact with me. I want unsaved people to get some of the joy-juice spilled on them when they are around me.

The fruit of the Spirit is joy. We are commanded to be joyful. Philippians 4:4 says, "Rejoice in the Lord always." First Thessalonians 5:16 says, "Be joyful always." It's a standing order for the Christian. You ask, "How?" By obeying the commands from the Bible, joy pours into our hearts and bubbles over to the lives of others.

If the Holy Spirit is in your heart, there's a reservoir of joy in you. To be filled with the Spirit is to be filled with joy. Acts 13:52 says, "And the disciples were filled with joy and with the Holy Spirit." As we yield to the Holy Spirit's control, this reservoir is released. Joy floats up to the top. Don't take for granted these wonderful moments when the joy of the Lord bubbles up on the inside and then overflows on the outside. We are told that Jesus "rejoiced in spirit." What did he do? He said, "I praise you, Father" (Luke 10:21). Be thankful for those wonderful times when the joy of the Lord is down in your heart and out in your life.

Huhmmmmmmm! The joy of the Lord is unspeakable and full of glory. That's better than a peach going down your throat and running down your chin! Now that's just peachy!

CHAPTER 5

A FRESH SLICE OF PEACE

"We're gonna have a watermelon cutting!" In the hot summertime, that's music to my ears. What's better than a watermelon cutting at a church fellowship or a family gathering? A juicy slice of watermelon and hot summer days just go together. I love watermelon.

Evidently watermelon originated in the desert areas of Africa. The 92 percent water content makes it a valuable source of water in desert areas. In hot weather, watermelon is indeed a cooling relief from hunger and thirst. The high water content also makes watermelon a popular food with dieters. It is also an excellent cleanser for the body.

In 1857 the Scottish missionary and explorer David Livingstone described an abundance of watermelons growing in the vast dry plateaus of the Kalahari Desert in Central South Africa. He noted they were variable in taste and that the natives and animals of the region ate them ravenously.[1]

Livingstone is legendary in the history of Christian missions. He spent thirty years as a missionary in Africa. During his sixteenth year there he faced the most dangerous situation of his missionary career. He was surrounded by hostile, angry natives. His life was in danger. Should he try to escape in the night? Well, something happened that night which soothed his spirit and changed his mind, giving him a peace in his peril. Was it a slice of watermelon? I'll tell you later.

"The fruit of the Spirit is . . . peace." There are few things people have sought as much as peace. Our world desperately longs for it. Have you heard about peace lately? The word is on the lips of virtually every world leader. Peace is a topic of conversation on MSNBC, CNN, and FOX News almost every night. It's almost as if the world pays lip service to peace, but do we ever achieve it? No way!

People are seeking inner peace. Peace of mind. Peace of heart. People look for peace in many places. Some search for peace in a drink. Others look for it in a sexual escapade. Still others search for peace in a mountain of pills. Pressured business leaders look for peace. Wounded wives seek peace to calm themselves. There's an irony to it all, don't you think? Our generation has sought peace more than any other, yet we seem to have found less peace than any previous generation. You've heard of heat-seeking missiles? Well, our generation is full of peace-seeking people!

Peace is one of the great words of the Bible. The Old Testament word is *Shalom*. If you are ever in Israel and don't know what to say, try "Shalom," meaning "a desire or prayer that all is well with you." The word itself actually carries the idea to make complete. It means "wholeness or a total well-being." The idea is that things are under control.

One of the names of God in the Old Testament is *Jehovah Shalom*, meaning God's got it all together. How can we tell? We see this completeness in his creation. There is a sense of wholeness about it. Sunrise and sunset are predictable. Seedtime and harvest are on time. God is the God of wholeness. The God who has things under control. The God of peace.

The New Testament word for peace basically means "to bind together." *Peace* occurs eighty-eight times in the New Testament. Many of the letters of the New Testament begin with "Grace and peace." *Peace*, in the New Testament, really means "tranquility or serenity." For example, think of the peace a country enjoys under the just or benevolent government of a good ruler. So peace means "that tranquil serenity of heart which comes of the all-pervading consciousness that our times are in the hands of God."[2]

We often describe peace using a negative framework: peace is the absence of war, strife, or violence. But peace is much more than this. It is not merely the absence of problems. It is the presence of Jesus. Peterson says that New Testament peace is "the realization that God works through the disparities and contradictions of my experience and brings them into harmony."[3]

Oswald Sanders further says that peace is "the inner tranquility and harmony enjoyed by the believer who is living in conformity to the will of God."[4]

What's the big deal here? Well, this helps us understand that peace is independent of what is going on outside. Peace is harmony and oneness with God's purposes. Remember that Jesus, the night before the cross, talked about his peace. So his peace was not something external. Outside, there was treachery, betrayal, violence, and pain. But his peace was deep within his heart.

There's a major connection between love, joy, and peace. Makes me think of the tie between faith, hope, and love. Timothy George says, "Love is the foundation; joy the superstructure; peace the crown of all."[5] How about a fresh slice of peace?

Peace Is a Gift

Jesus had a lot to say about peace, especially the night before the cross. As he gathered with his disciples in the closing hours, he mentioned peace several times. In John 14:27 he says, "Peace I leave with you; my peace I give you. I do not give to you as the world gives. Do not let your hearts be troubled and do not be afraid."

He continues in John 16:33, "I have told you these things, so that in me you may have peace. In this world you will have trouble. But take heart! I have overcome the world."

After his death and resurrection he mentions peace three times to his disciples (John 20:19, 21, 26). Jesus promises to give us peace. This peace is a gift.

Romans 5:1 makes all this clear. It says, "Therefore, since we have been justified through faith, we have peace with God through our Lord Jesus Christ."

Peace with God. Like the sound of that? Well, it comes from salvation. Remember the greetings of many New Testament letters? Grace, then peace? The order is significant. Think of two sisters. Peace is younger, grace is older. Grace always is first, then comes peace. Always. It's never reversed. People look for peace, but if they have not received God's grace, they won't find it. Peace comes after you experience grace.

This gift of peace can only come from God. He is indeed Jehovah Shalom, the God of Peace, and the New Testament frequently refers to him that way (see Rom. 15:33; 16:20; 2 Cor. 13:11; Phil. 4:9; 1 Thess. 5:23; Heb. 13:20).

So how do we get this peace? God gives it to us only through Jesus Christ. Romans 5:1 specifically says it is *through our Lord Jesus Christ.* Ephesians 2:14 says that *Jesus is our peace.* Sin created hostility between God and us. This hostility toward God produces conflict in our hearts. Get the picture? Sin is the disruptive factor. Sin brings the conflict. Sin creates the hostility. It makes us God's enemies. How do we deal with that? Enter—the gospel! At the cross Jesus dealt with the sin that separates us from God. Colossians 1:20 says, "And through him to reconcile to himself all things, whether things on earth or things in heaven, by making peace through his blood, shed on the cross."

When I was younger I used to hear the old-timers say, "Have you made your peace with God?" The truth is, we can't. More truth is, we don't have to. Jesus has already done it! The blood of Christ settled the sin grievance between man and God.

Remember Livingstone? Well, one time he was negotiating with an African chief about establishing peace between his tribe and an enemy tribe. The African chief said to Livingstone, "How can I be at peace with them while they still hold my son prisoner?" Good question. How can people expect to find peace with God when they reject his Son? Job 22:21 says, "Submit to God and be at peace with him." Peace with God is already out there. It has been achieved by the finished work of Jesus Christ on the cross. Only when we are justified by faith can we accept peace with God. Remember, peace is out there.

Second Thessalonians 3:16 says, "the Lord of peace himself give you peace." Hey, I'm glad I'm a preacher. I get to preach a gospel of peace (Rom. 10:15). As I preach what Christ did on the cross, people who are battling with God and experiencing chaos in their hearts can receive by faith what Christ did at the cross. When they do, they receive as a gift this wonderful peace with God. How about another fresh slice of peace?

Peace Is a Grace

Peace is a gift, but it is also one of the graces of the Spirit. It results from the work of the Holy Spirit in our hearts and his control in our relationships with other people. Saved people have the choice to enjoy peace with God. God's peace can be deposited in the bank of their hearts. Philippians 4:7 talks about the *peace of God*. Many believers do not have this peace. Do you know any? The Holy Spirit can spread this God-given peace into every area of a believer's heart. It's a personal and internal peace that not only deals with saving the soul but also with living life. All Christians can choose peace. The potential is there.

So what does peace really mean? It means to join together. It's the opposite of worry. Worry pulls apart. Do you ever worry? When you worry, your mind and heart are pulled apart. You think one way, but feel another. Hello! That means conflict! But a state of calm, a supernatural rest in the heart is available to a Christian.

Ever drive a car without shock absorbers? One night I borrowed a car from a friend. I soon found out the car had no shock absorbers. Interesting ride! Think of God's peace like shock absorbers on a car. His peace enables a smooth ride over life's bumpy roads.

Look at Philippians 4:7. What does it say about this peace of God? We are told it passes all understanding, meaning it is incredible. Many believers testify that in the midst of unbelievably turbulent situations, they have experienced deep peace in their hearts. They can't explain it. It was just there. It is hard to put into words just how incredible this peace is. Have you heard that twenty-five feet below the ocean's surface there is a calm untouched by the howling winds and churning waves on the surface? Christians can choose to experience this incredible peace like this calm in the ocean.

James Merritt tells of some Korean Christians who were going through persecution. They responded by saying, "We are just like nails. The harder you drive us, the deeper you drive us. And the deeper you drive us, the more peaceful it becomes."

Peace of God "will guard your hearts and minds." God's peace in the heart is invincible. Do you get the picture? Think of a Roman guard standing watch. He calls out through the night, "It's 11:00 P.M. and all is well." When an unfamiliar person approaches he calls, "Who goes there?" The peace of God is not only a believer's possession; it is also a believer's protection. We have a choice, and choosing peace keeps the heart from worrying in hard times.

The peace of God is also available to us because it is "in Christ." His peace is available to us in every situation and circumstance. Would you like this peace of God on a daily basis? Here's how to get it.

Isaiah 26:3 (KJV) says, "Thou wilt keep him in perfect peace, whose mind is stayed on thee." The word *stayed* carries the idea of placing, laying upon, or resting upon. It is used also in Isaiah 48:2 and the Song of Solomon 2:5. When we rest our minds upon the person and character of God, we can experience his peace. Choose to keep your life focused on the Lord and peace will be the result.

Psalm 119:165 says, "Great peace have they who love your law." Isaiah 48:18 says, "your peace would have been like a river." What's that all about? Great peace. Peace like a river. Sound interesting? As we read and heed God's Word in our lives, peace comes.

Dr. Smiley Blanton, director of the American Foundation of Religion and Psychiatry, was once asked if he read the Bible? His reply is most interesting. "I not only read it, I study it. It's the greatest textbook on human behavior ever put together. If people would just absorb its message, a lot of us psychiatrists could close our offices and go fishing."[6] Daily Bible reading brings great peace to the heart. Peace also carries the idea of wholeness or completeness in life. In the Bible we learn principles of wholeness. For instance, think about "love your neighbor." Or "Don't worry about tomorrow." And "the truth will make you free." There are countless other truths that contribute to making life whole. The most well-adjusted people I know are Christians who search the Scriptures daily to find and to obey God's truths.

Here's another good one. "Let the peace of Christ rule in your hearts" (Col. 3:15). The word *rule* means to "act as an umpire." Think baseball! Allow God's peace to be the referee in your heart. Think about your personal holiness before you let anything into your life. Say, "You're out!" to a bad movie or "You're safe!" to a good book. The psychologist William James said that every sensation or contact we have with the world leaves a trace among our ten billion brain cells. These traces are permanent and continually accumulate in our brains. The total of these sensations, according to James, is our personality and character. He then says that everything we do makes it easier to do the same thing again.[7] So more and more of God's peace can come into our lives as we allow that peace to rule. Get it? By consciously acting upon the peace we now have, we can expect more of God's peace to guide and direct our lives. I like it!

The peace of God is also relational or external. Peace should be a vital ingredient in our relationships with other people. Romans 14:19 makes it clear: "Let us therefore make every effort to do what leads to peace and to mutual edification." Timothy George says, "We are to do all we can to do what leads to peace and mutual edification."[8]

It is our choice to experience peace with believers. Of all people, Christians should have peaceful relationships with one another. Our common relationship to Jesus Christ provides a basis for this peace. Ephesians 2:14–17 teaches that Christ has broken down the walls that separate us from one another, making peace possible. What walls? Walls of race, walls of economic status, and walls of culture have all been broken down by Christ. Whatever race, economic status, or cultural atmosphere you come from, God's peace in your heart can give you peace with other believers.

Have you ever known anyone hard to get along with? I bet Paul was before he became a Christian. The unsaved Paul certainly had knowledge and zeal. But if anyone had something else to say, he'd kill them! What was Paul's trouble? He was a walking civil war. There was great conflict on the inside. After his conversion, God's peace ruled in his heart. Then he loved people. He wanted to help and bless them. This is why we read so much about his appreciation for his coworkers. Read Romans 16 again. Look at the long list of people Paul names who shared ministry with him. Do you sense the great peace he feels with them? The same is true for many of us who have been serving the Lord a long time. Though we differ in so many ways, the presence of God's peace in our hearts enables us to work harmoniously and lovingly with one another. If only the world's nations could work with this peace!

A human heart filled with God's peace makes it possible to have peace with others. Yet few people find peace! Conflict is everywhere. On the job, at school, and especially at home, there is turmoil. What do people encounter when they cross your path or my path? People should get a delicious taste of peace when they are around us. Look at Romans 14:19 again,

"Let us therefore make every effort to do what leads to peace." Thomas à Kempis said, "All desire peace, but few desire those things which make for peace."[9]

When Jesus met people, he brought them peace. I love it when Jesus said to people, "Go in peace" (Luke 7:50). This is a literal translation of what he said. When people come to Christ, they come into an atmosphere where peace is an option they can choose. How about another slice of peace?

Peace Is a Goal

We can choose peace with God because Christ paid the penalty for our sins. We can have peace with ourselves because he clears us from guilt and drains the inner conflict from our hearts. We can have peace with others because the Holy Spirit seeks to produce this peace in our personal relationships. We are free to seek peace. Hebrews 12:14 encourages, "Make every effort to live in peace with all men and to be holy; without holiness no one will see the Lord." Christians are to be peacemakers. Jesus said, "Blessed are the peacemakers: for they shall be called the children of God" (Matt. 5:9 KJV). That's peacemakers, not peacebreakers. Are you a peacemaker? If you are Spirit-filled, you are. What is an evidence that you are a Spirit-filled believer? How about being a peacemaker?

Ah, family life. We definitely need peace there! When Paul encourages us to let the peace of God rule in our hearts in Colossians 3:15, he says this in the context of his statements about family. How about 1 Corinthians 7? Here Paul discusses the whole issue of marriage, and right in the middle of it he says, "God has called us to live in peace" (v. 15).

A group of men were surveyed about their home life. They were asked what men wanted most? The answer might surprise you. Most of the men surveyed said they wanted peace at home. Our homes should be havens of rest. When we allow the Holy Spirit to control family life, we choose to experience peace.

What about church? Do we need peace there? Uh-huh! First Corinthians 14:33 says, "For God is not a God of disorder but of peace. As in all the congregations of the saints." God wants peace in his church. The Bible is pretty rough on disturbers of peace in the church. When peace is disrupted in a church, that means the devil's work is going on. We know that walking in the flesh produces strife and walking after the Spirit produces peace. Paul comes down pretty hard on the peacebreakers. He says in Romans 16:17–18 that we are to mark these troublemakers and to avoid them.

The early church experienced tensions. There was tension between Jews and Gentiles. For years, they had detested one another. But life in the church was to be different. They were "to keep the unity of the Spirit through the bond of peace" (Eph. 4:3). The lesson here is relevant to Christians today. When we have conflicts, we should show the love of Jesus. This goes a long way toward creating peace.

It is not always easy to have peace with other people, is it? Maybe this is why Paul said in Romans 12:18, "If it is possible, as far as it depends on you, live at peace with everyone." So what does that mean? While it may not be possible to have peace with everyone, be sure that you are not the problem. Always be a peacemaker, a peaceseeker, never a peacebreaker.

Think globally! We should also seek peace in our world. Our world does seek peace, but it cannot find it. Evil people simply do not know the way of peace. Romans 3:17 makes it clear that peace is not available to those who do not know the Lord. Of course, a false peace can exist. Think about the Pax Romana, the Roman peace during the time of Christ. But it was a false peace. It was a peace of domination. There was no peace in the hearts of the people. Rome dictated all of life. This was not peace. It was misery.

Even today, there is a false peace. It lets vices go unchecked and violence go without restraint. This is not peace. This is utter chaos.

What can we do? All we can! We should preach the gospel of peace (Eph. 6:15). We should pray for our leaders that peace might be realized. I think often of our responsibility as cited in 1 Timothy 2:1–4. We are told that we should pray for our leaders, "that we may live peaceful and quiet lives in all godliness and holiness" (v. 2).

I saw a bumper sticker the other day that said, "Visualize world peace." Can thinking about it make it happen? Excuse me, that's not how world peace comes about, now or ever. So what will ultimately bring peace to the world? The return of the Prince of Peace (Isa. 9:6). There will be no peace on earth until Jesus, the Prince of Peace, comes back. Of course there is the peace that develops in individual hearts and the peace between people who have the same heart experience. This is what Jesus meant when he said, "Glory to God in the highest, and on earth peace to men on whom his favor rests" (Luke 2:14).

Only when Jesus comes to earth again will we enjoy peace here. Until then, we should seek to live in as much peace as possible. And daily we should be praying for the return of Jesus Christ.

A speaker at a Bible conference shared that the return of Christ was a great prayer of the early church. He mentioned that the word *maranatha* ("the Lord is coming") was a key word between believers. The morning after the conference two older ladies met one another for breakfast. One of them said to the other, "Marijuana, sister, marijuana." Well, "Maranatha! Come Lord Jesus." Why? Because when Jesus comes, peace on earth will come. Maranatha!

Back to David Livingstone. The night was perilous. What would he do? That night Livingstone, surrounded by hostile natives, found an incredible, unbelievable calm. He wrote about it in his diary on January 14, 1856. He recorded that he read the promise, "Lo, I am with you alway, even unto the end of the world" (Matt. 28:20 KJV). Then he said, "It is the word of a gentleman of the most strict and sacred honor, so there's an end to it. I will not cross furtively tonight as I intended. Should such a man as I flee? Nay, verily, I shall take observations for latitude tonight, though they may be the last. I feel QUITE CALM NOW, THANK GOD!"[10]

What carried Livingstone through the crisis? A slice of watermelon? No. A slice of peace! You, too, can choose this peace.

Jesus stood on the deck of the ship. The storm was raging all around. He spoke the words *peace, be still*. The wind ceased blowing. The waves laid down like whipped puppies at his feet. There was great calm. Are the winds blowing in your life? Are the waves threatening to overwhelm you? Jesus can bring peace to your heart. His peace can calm the angry storms. The choice is yours.

We are actually commanded as Christians to have this peace. How do we get it? Do we rush to the hardware store and buy a gallon of peace? Or do we head for the bar and get a fifth of peace? Or do we go to the cloth shop and purchase a yard of peace? I don't think so. There's only one place we can get peace. Philippians 4:9 says, "And the God of peace will be with you." The peace of God comes only from the God of peace. He has a monopoly on it. He has an abundant supply. Have a fresh slice of peace!

CHAPTER 6

LOOKING FOR MR. SWEETBAR

Do you like candy bars? I do! Yep, I'll eat all kinds. I like Baby Ruths. I love Butterfingers. I like Mr. Goodbars. But my favorite of all is the Snickers bar. That's really what turns me on! Nothing like it. One caution: don't look at the fat content! You'll have a seizure. Fortunately, another candy is not as loaded. Have you ever heard of Mr. Sweetbar? Read on.

Have you ever eaten a date? Did you know dates are called "candy that grows on trees." A date is a sweet, chewy fruit. Imagine a new candy bar made with milk chocolate and dates. Wouldn't that be good? I'd call such a confection the Mr. Sweetbar. It would be sweet to the taste but also would help the eater day by day. How? Read on!

Date trees live very long lives. Date palms produce a new section of leaves every year. They don't start bearing fruit until the fourth year. And they are most productive when they are about eighty years of age. Dates are longsuffering. They produce an average of one hundred pounds of fruit annually.[1] This sweet date candy is produced only by patience.

The fruit of the Spirit is patience. Think of patience as the candy bar of the Spirit, a Mr. Sweetbar. The Greek word is really made up of two words. The first *makro* means slow. The other *thumos* means wrath. So, it means "to be of long wrath." The idea is handling anger slowly. In other words, it means "having a slow fuse." Barclay says it is "a kind of conquering patience."[2] Think of being slow to right wrongs or to be self-restrained.

Patience doesn't mean an absence of anger. Rather, the emphasis is on how to handle one's anger. Briscoe suggests that it is anger properly handled.[3] The Bible tells us that anger is not always wrong. Jesus was angry. Mark 3:5 says, "He looked around at them in anger and, deeply distressed at their stubborn hearts . . . ." Ephesians 4:26 tells us, "In your anger do not sin: Do not let the sun go down while you are still angry." The key is not whether one is angry, but what one does with the anger.

Not enough people these days are eating Mr. Sweetbars. Today it's all about quick retribution. If you don't like it, just push DELETE. Others do something to you, shoot them a hot E-mail. If people are in the way, take a gun and wipe them out. It's an impatient age. Instant gratification is where it's at. We see the "now-ness" of our lives all around. There are instant soups and coffees. Instant shaving creams and medicine. Even instant justice. How about the Chia pet? It grows hair instantly! Criswell says, "In a world of speed, we are to be slow to take offense."[4]

Unfortunately, we are not born with a lot of patience. The Holy Spirit has to give it to us. We all need patience. Wouldn't you like to be more like the little boy at the end of the escalator in the department store? He was watching the moving rail as it came by. A sales lady asked, "Son, are you lost?"

"No, ma'am. I'm just waiting for my chewing gum to come back."

Patience is an attribute of God. This word is all about his nature and his character. Exodus 34:6 says, "And he passed in front of Moses, proclaiming, 'The LORD, the LORD, the compassionate and gracious God, slow to anger, abounding in love and faithfulness'" (also see Neh. 9:17; Ps. 86:15; 103:8; 145:8). It was the longsuffering of God that held back his wrath before the flood. "Who disobeyed long ago when God waited patiently in the days of Noah while the ark was being built" (1 Pet. 3:20).

Because of his patience, the second coming of Christ has not yet taken place. "The Lord is not slow in keeping his promise, as some understand slowness. He is patient with you, not wanting anyone to perish, but everyone to come to repentance" (2 Pet. 3:9). God is patient with us. He wants people to repent. The day of judgment and wrath will be severe and final. But until then, God is holding back. Pleading. Enduring. God is patient. Barclay says, "If God had been as man He would have taken His hand and wiped out this world long ago. But, God has that patience which bears with all our sinning and which will not cast us off."[5]

Jesus' patience should be our pattern. "But for that very reason I was shown mercy so that in me, the worst of sinners, Christ Jesus might display his unlimited patience as an example for those who would believe on him and receive eternal life" (1 Tim. 1:16). His patience enabled him to pray on the cross "Father, forgive them . . . ." Second Thessalonians 3:5 again notes the patience of Christ, "May the Lord direct your hearts into God's love and Christ's perseverance."

Because God has been patient with us, we should show this grace to others. People need to see patience produced by the Holy Spirit in our lives. Ephesians 4:2 urges that we are to "be patient, bearing with one another in love."

Now let's take a few bites of a Mr. Sweetbar. We need this sweet SpiritFruit for several reasons.

Wrestle with Problems

Patience enables us to persevere bravely on a bad day or during longer hardships. Paul showed great patience. In 2 Corinthians 6:4ff, Paul indicates that he approved himself "as servants of God . . . in purity, understanding, patience, and kindness; in the Holy Spirit and in sincere love." Look at the use of the word *in*. "In troubles, hardships and distresses." The question is basically what are you *in*? How did Paul handle being *in* such circumstances? By "purity, understanding, patience." How can you make it through your difficult problems? Patience is certainly one way.

Many problems in life call for longsuffering. "Brothers, as an example of patience in the face of suffering, take the prophets who spoke in the name of the Lord" (James 5:10). James gives us the example of Job. Think of all Job suffered. His afflictions are known worldwide.

We often ask why we have afflictions and sufferings. Here are several suggestions why these afflictions may come. They come to discipline us. "Will your courage endure or your hands be strong in the day I deal with you? I the LORD have spoken, and I will do it" (Ezek. 22:14). Also, Hebrews 12:5–13 indicates that God uses afflictions and sufferings at times to chastise us and draw us back into fellowship with him.

Or sometimes God allows afflictions and sufferings to stretch us. "It was good for me to be afflicted / so that I might learn your decrees" (Ps. 119:71). Ian Thomas said, "Boys will be boys, but be patient and boys will be men."

Sometimes God uses suffering to direct us. Think of the afflictions of Joseph. When it was all over Joseph realized "God meant it for good"

(Gen. 50:20 NASB). So when hard times come, ask the Holy Spirit to give you patience and deal with it.

We live under constant pressure, and patience can help us handle it. Really, that's what it's all about. Patience is love under pressure. James uses the prophets as an example of patience under pressure (James 5:10). We need the same patience today. There is pressure everywhere today—pressures of business deals, family pressures, peer pressures. All these pressures bring nervous tension and stress. But the Holy Spirit will give us patience if we ask.

We also need patience to handle failures that come our way. Sometimes our goals are not achieved. We fail to realize our ambitions. But we should be slow to become angry and frustrated by them. Robert Frost waited a long time before his poetry made him famous. In fact, it was thirty-nine years before he sold one volume of his poems. But his patience paid off. His poems were translated into twenty-two languages and his poetry won a Pulitzer Prize four times. Hang in there.

Sometimes it's not the big things that get us, but the little things. Satan often is like a woodpecker pecking away at us day by day. Have you ever had days when life seems to come unglued because of the little things? I have! The Holy Spirit can help us bear the little trials and annoyances of life with calm and serenity of spirit. Even in traffic! One writer put it this way: "I thought if defeat came at all, it would be a big bold definite joust with a cause or a name. And it came. I had not thought the daily skirmish with a few details, worthwhile: and so I turned my back upon them year on year; until one day a million minutia blanketed together rose up and overwhelmed me."[6]

Yes, the Holy Spirit produces patience in our lives. But that does not mean we are automatically freed from trials. We're supposed to take a bite of the Mr. Sweetbar during the trials. Get it?

I'm still learning to work my computer. Just a stroke and HELP is on the way! In the Christian life God has given us the powerful key of PRAYER. Do you have trials going on? Then, hit the key of PRAYER and Jesus is instantly on the scene! Simon Peter was sinking in the sea. He prayed one of the shortest prayers on record, "Lord, save me!" (Matt. 14:30). Jesus instantly reached out and rescued him. Someone said, "When you come to the end of the rope, tie a prayer knot and hang on!"

So the Holy Spirit uses the very problems we wrestle with to develop the grace of patience in us.

Work with People

We do not live or work in a vacuum. Unless you are a hermit (and I've known a few), you must relate to other people. Is that easy? Not really. Patience handles the offenses and injuries coming from others. Timothy George says it is "the ability to put up with other people even when it is not easy to do."[7] That might be every day for you. Barclay quotes Chrysostom: "Longsuffering is the grace of the man who could revenge himself and does not."[8]

The Bible teaches that God is patient with people—even the undeserving. Romans 9:22 says, "What if God, choosing to show his wrath and make his power known, bore with great patience the objects of his wrath—prepared for destruction?"

Often, we are not as patient with people as we ought to be. Most of us have short fuses. We blow at the slightest delay or disturbance. We get too irritated too quickly. But the Holy Spirit can produce in our lives a God-like patience toward other people. In fact, he may even use people to help us become more patient! How's that for living God's way?

A certain devout maiden asked Athanasius to help her cultivate the grace of patience. Athanasius gave her a poor widow as a companion. The widow was cross, irritable, intolerable, and constantly complaining. The young maiden was provided every opportunity she needed to practice patience![9]

The Holy Spirit can enable us to be patient with people regardless of how unreasonable, unkind, and unloving they are. Our tendency is to respond with righteous indignation. Often we don't act—we react. We usually react with anger. The Holy Spirit can help us act with patience instead of reacting with hostility.

A wicked tyrant said to a Christian whom he held in prison, "What can Christ do for you now?" "He can help me forgive you," the Christian said.

Patience is a trait especially needed by Christian preachers and teachers today. Second Timothy 3:10–11 says, "You, however, know all about my teaching, my way of life, my purpose, faith, patience, love, endurance, persecutions, sufferings." Also, 2 Timothy 4:2 says, "Preach the Word; be prepared in season and out of season; correct, rebuke and encourage—with great patience and careful instruction." Dealing with people on the basis of longsuffering is a mark of mature spiritual leadership. Second Corinthians 12:12 says, "The things that mark an apostle—signs, wonders and miracles—were done among you with great perseverance."

Patience is an essential trait you must possess to be a spiritual leader. I heard recently about a pastor who was encountering difficulties in dealing with his church members. "They said they wanted a pastor for the sheep," he said, "but what they really need is a zookeeper for the animals." Teachers, you may feel the same way!

When I read of Jesus I can see his patience. He was patient, even with his own disciples. Think of all the stuff he put up with. Don't you know it tried the patience of Jesus when Simon Peter constantly put his foot in his mouth saying stupid things? Jesus showed patience with the hot tempers of James and John. They were hostile and rude. The disciples were slow to catch on to things he taught. Much of it passed right over their heads. Yet Jesus, as the Master Teacher, was patient with them.

Think of our Lord's patience with people in general. Many times people infringed on his time. Exhausted, needing rest, he couldn't get away from them. Yet there is no occasion where Jesus was short-tempered and unkind to people.

Jesus was even patient with his enemies. Remember Judas? Jesus endured the treachery of Judas. Even to the very end Jesus reached out to Judas. He showed patience to those who tried to discredit him and to destroy him. What an example for us!

Even when others do us wrong, we should show patience. How do you react when people mistreat you? I know my own tendency. I tend to defend myself. But Romans 12:19 clearly says, "Do not take revenge, my friends, but leave room for God's wrath, for it is written: 'It is mine to avenge; I will repay,' says the Lord." Patience enables us to leave the matter in the hands of God and let it go.

David had to deal with Saul. He spent years working for a spear-throwing king. Saul's jealousy almost drove him to insanity. His unfairness and injustice to David was tragic. Yet through it all David was patient with Saul. David had many opportunities to do Saul harm, yet David never touched God's anointed. How could he be so patient? First Samuel 30:6 says, "David found strength in the Lord his God." We can turn to the Lord for the same kind of encouragement. That encouragement from God enables us to be patient as we relate to people.

Patience is greatly needed in the home. It is easier to lose our patience at home more quickly than anywhere else, don't you think? Tragic, but true, the people you love the most will call for the most patience. Why is that? Home is where we really are what we are. Our true selves come out at home. We throw off our shoes, flop back in our easy chair, and hit the Diet Coke! We are often too impatient and unkind. Husband and wife can be short-tempered with each other. Brothers and sisters can be quick to blame each other. We really need the grace of patience to relate well with our family members. Many family troubles come from our impatient words and actions.

We also need patience at our jobs and in our social relationships. If we are impatient, we may misjudge the situation. Drescher shares a familiar story told by the Georgia evangelist Sam Jones. A group of people were on a train. It was hot, the journey was long, and everyone was tired. A man was trying to handle his crying baby. The little one just seemed to cry louder and louder. One exasperated man finally blurted out, "Why don't you take that baby to its mother?" The man replied, "I'm sorry. I'm doing my best. I can't take it to its mother. My baby's mother is in a casket in the baggage car." There was an uncomfortable silence. The man who asked the question apologized for his impatient, unkind words. Then he took the child and tended it for the rest of the journey.[10]

Do we need patience at church? You bet! Church is a unique atmosphere for expressing patience. Ephesians 4:2 emphasizes that we are to "be patient, bearing with one another in love." First Thessalonians 5:14 emphasizes that we are to "be patient with everyone." Sometimes we show our patience not only in what we do but also by what we do not do.

Simon Peter was feeling especially spiritual. The Jews allowed forgiveness of a person three times. Peter said, "I'll double that then add one." "Lord, how often should I forgive? Seven times?" He was proud of himself. He thought he was a big man. Then Jesus gave the shocker: "Not seven times. Seven times seventy!" Jesus was saying we must learn to be patient.

Patience is not a sign of weakness. Jesus was patient on the cross. In fact, we are told that he "endured the cross" (Heb. 12:2). Jesus could have called down twelve legions of angels. But what did he do? He prayed for those who crucified him. That's where our salvation comes from. Second Peter 3:15 says, "Bear in mind that our Lord's patience means salvation." Displaying the grace of patience in your life may lead someone else to Christ. Your patience in dealing with people may convince others that your faith is the real deal.

A phone operator commented to a fellow operator, "That's the most patient man I have ever dealt with. I called the wrong number four times. He just kindly said to me, 'Try again.' I wonder who he is?" Her fellow operator said, "That's my preacher." The first operator said, "I'm going to hear him preach."[11]

When Stanley found Livingstone in Africa, he was greatly impressed. Livingstone never spoke to him about spiritual things. But Stanley watched the old missionary deal with the African people with love and patience. He wrote, "When I saw that unwearied patience, that unflagging zeal with those enlightened children of Africa, I became a Christian at his side, though he never spoke a word to me about it."[12]

Like most of the other graces of the Spirit, patience is a product of love.

First Corinthians 13:4 says, "Love is patient." Because God helps us love people, he can also help us be patient with them.

Wait with Promises

Would it surprise you if I said there are times when we need patience with our Lord? God has his own timetable. Too often we say, "Hurry up, please!" God says, "Patience." Hebrews 10:36 says, "You need to persevere so that when you have done the will of God, you will receive what he has promised." Abraham is an example of a person waiting for the promises of God. Hebrews 6:15 says, "And so after waiting patiently, Abraham received what was promised."

God quite often plans much bigger for our lives than we plan for our own. He's a big-picture God. I don't know who said it, but it is true: God's delays are not his denials. George Mueller, the great prayer warrior and friend of children, prayed almost sixty years for a friend's salvation. The man came to Christ at Mueller's funeral. That's patience.

We have the promise that God is working in our lives to help us be more patient. When we are impatient we cannot see the Holy Spirit's work in us. One time a missionary did not receive his monthly check. He was seriously ill. He had no money to buy food. So he lived on oatmeal and canned milk. But he got better. His check arrived thirty days late. On furlough he visited his doctor and told him the situation. The doctor asked the nature of his illness. He had experienced digestive problems. The doctor said, "If your check had arrived on time, you would be dead now. The very best treatment for your illness was a thirty-day oatmeal diet."[13] We do not always understand what God is doing in our lives. We need to be patient and wait for his promises.

New Testament teachings on patience show that a strong dose of hope is in the mixture. Romans 8:25 says, "But if we hope for what we do not yet have, we wait for it patiently." God is at work, and that makes our future promising. The familiar saying, "The future is as bright as the promises of God," is certainly true. So we really ought to be patient. Romans 2:7 says, "To those who by persistence in doing good seek glory, honor and immortality, he will give eternal life." James 5:7 says, "Be patient, then, brothers, until the Lord's coming." James uses a farmer as an illustration of patience. Why? One simple reason. The farmer has the promise of the harvest! Don't you see? God has a harvest in mind for your life. Be patient. One day the glorious crops will come in!

Look at Hebrews 10:36 again. "You need to persevere so that when you have done the will of God, you will receive what he has promised." There's a lot involved in waiting for the promises of God to come. First of all, there is the trust factor. Hebrews 6:12 says, "We do not want you to become lazy, but to imitate those who through faith and patience inherit what has been promised." We must believe the promises of God. How? By having confidence in God's character. God is who he says he is. God will do what he says he will do. Therefore, let us trust his promises.

Next, there is the time factor. That's where longsuffering comes in. Our temptation is to grow impatient. A member of my church was recently going through a very difficult family problem. Great injustice was being done. The member said to me with real hurt in his voice, "Preacher, what about the promises?" I was able to remind him of Hebrews 10:36. We need patience to wait on the Lord. We need to allow the time to cause our patience to develop fully.

Finally, there is the thrill factor when we receive the promise! Then the patience pays off! Are you holding on to a promise from God? Keep holding on! Down the road God's promises will come through. You will be so glad you have been patient.

Remember, patience is commanded in the Scriptures. James 5:8 commands, "Be patient." Then, he adds an incentive, "The Lord's coming is near." To be patient means to be driven to God in prayer. Our job is to ask the Holy Spirit to produce this sweet fruit like dates in our lives.

Colossians 3:12 says that we are to "clothe yourselves with . . . patience" as a part of our Christian wardrobe. As we ask the Holy Spirit to produce this grace in our lives, then by faith we *put it on*. Guess what! You are going to look really good in your new patient outfit.

Patience is like a delicious candy bar. Take a big bite of Mr. Sweetbar.

Ummmmm! Have another bite. It will be sweet to your taste and healthy to your soul!

As I was writing this book, Walter Payton, perhaps the greatest running back in the history of football, died at the young age of forty-five. He was known as "Sweetness." He was a sweet runner. But, even better, a sweet person. In his last days, as he waited in vain for a liver transplant, he demonstrated the sweet trait of patience. God help us to also give evidence as we take regular bites of Mr. Sweetbar!

CHAPTER 7

IS KINDNESS REALLY *ALL THAT?*

"Who told her she was *all that?*" the woman asked her friend at the supermarket the other day. Apparently, they were having a conversation about a friend of theirs who had just received a big job promotion. There they stood beside the lettuce. It did not sound like a friendly conversation. So I quickly picked out my tomato and left them talking in the produce section.

Amazing, isn't it? You can learn so much about human nature just by listening to people around you. The conversation I heard that day wasn't a very kind one. It sounded to me like there was some major jealousy going on. But it's the *all that* phrase that stuck out to me. I've since learned it's another one of these hip expressions meaning "the best" or "the coolest." I went home and asked Janet if the tomato I picked out was *all that*. She just gave me one of those looks.

But it's really true. We see and hear so little kindness as we deal with one another on a daily basis. Christians may be the worst offenders. We're supposed to display God's kindness to others, but instead we're so busy or preoccupied that we don't. Kindness is the fruit of the Spirit that really is *all that*. It is what makes or breaks our Christian witness.

Have you ever eaten a fig? OK, so figs may not be the most popular or most exotic fruit, but I like them. Actually, figs are special. This exotic pear-shaped fruit is prized for its rich, sweet, and alluring taste. Figs are almost addictive. Perhaps this is because of their high sugar content. I like them best in the middle of a delicious Fig Newton cookie! I know, I know, Fat Gram City! It's just that I've loved them since I was a kid.

Figs can be very healthy. They are known for their restorative powers. Pliny, the Roman naturalist, wrote, "Figs are restorative, and the best food that can be taken by those who are brought low by long sickness . . . wrestlers and champions were in times past fed with figs."[1] Figs provide energy and vitality. If you do not drink milk, add figs to your regular diet, because they are a very good source of calcium.

Anyway, figs are all over the Bible. The fig is the first fruit mentioned in the Bible. Remember how Adam and Eve tried to cover their nakedness with fig leaves? If you have ever touched fig leaves, you know how uncomfortable and scratchy that would be! This reminds me of the wool trousers my mother used to buy for me when I was a boy. Talk about uncomfortable and scratchy? Fig leaves.

Figs are also used symbolically in the Bible. For example, the fig can represent the good life. Talking about "every man under his fig tree" (2 Kings 18:31) meant living a life of ease and leisure.

In addition, Jesus used the fig as a symbol of the nation of Israel. The blossoming fig tree in summer illustrates the restoration of Israel in the end-times.

So why all the talk about figs? Well, one Old Testament word for kindness also describes very good figs or figs that are *all that*! So there's the connection. In the physical world, figs provide the calcium normally derived from milk. When dealing with people and with relationships, we need nourishment from the milk of human kindness, don't we? Simply put, kindness is needed because it can heal and restore. Kindness can open a door for a positive witness for Christ when all other doors may be closed.

So what's up with kindness? It is another fruit of the Spirit, like patience and love. Unfortunately, we live in a culture where there isn't much kindness. Our age is more often characterized by rudeness, harshness, crudeness, and ugliness. Just think about traffic. Too often being kind is thought to show weakness. Ours is such a macho world. People do not want to be thought of as weak or soft. But kindness is a God-like trait because God is kind. To have the grace of kindness produced in our Christian life is to be more like God.

Some think kindness just won't work in our kind of world. It's a tough world, sometimes called dog-eat-dog. Get ahead at any cost. Climb over people in any way necessary to get what you want! Many are like Lady Macbeth, who feared her husband was "too full 'o the milk of human kindness."

But kindness is not weakness. It is a vital ingredient for successful interpersonal relationships. You say you're a Christian? Are your coworkers refreshed after being around your kindness?

> Life is mostly froth and bubble,
> Two things stand like stone,
> Kindness in another's trouble,
> Courage in your own.
> —Adam Lindsay Gordon

Briscoe says, "There is something classy about kindness."[2] I agree. "When I think of the charming people I know, it's surprising how often I find the chief of the qualities that make them so, is just that they are kind."[3]

In the Bible the word *kindness* is like a beautiful, ripe fig. Kindness is not mere sentimentality. It is stronger than that. In the Old Testament, it means "to bow the head." It carries the idea of treating courteously and appropriately.[4] We see kindness in the Old Testament as a characteristic of God, because God is kind in his dealings with people. Nehemiah 9:17 says, "But you are a forgiving God, gracious and compassionate, slow to anger and abounding in love . . ." Isaiah 40:11 says, ". . . He gently leads those that have young." God is a kind God. Does that surprise you? We get the idea that the Old Testament pictures God only as a stern, wrathful God. God is a God of justice and wrath, but he is also a loving, kind God.

The New Testament word for kindness refers to goodness of heart. So kindness is really a goodness that is kind. Barclay describes it as "a kindly disposition which expresses itself in deeds and words."[5] Drescher says, "Kindness is awareness of how the other feels, consideration of these feelings and adaptation of our attitudes, words, and behavior accordingly."[6] To be gracious to others is to treat them as God treats you. Ephesians 4:32 says, "Be kind and compassionate to one another, forgiving each other, just as in Christ God forgave you."

Kindness is not a normal trait to the human personality. While some by nature are kinder than others, the Bible says of the human race, "All have turned away, they have together become worthless; there is no one who does good, not even one" (Rom. 3:12). The Holy Spirit must produce this spiritual kindness in Christian's relationships with others. Let's pull a fig from the tree, or a Fig Newton from the box, and examine to see if kindness is *all that*.

Experiencing Kindness

God's kindness is all over the place! You can see it with all people (those who are his children and those who aren't). Luke 6:35 says, "But love your enemies, do good to them, and lend to them without expecting to get any thing back. Then your reward will be great, and you will be sons of the Most High, because he is kind to the ungrateful and wicked." First Peter 2:3 says, "Now that you have tasted that the Lord is good." Are you alive and breathing today? It is because of the kindness of God. Do you have a rational mind? Is your body healthy? It's all because of the kindness of God. Have you had the opportunity to know God in a personal way? It is because God has been kind to you.

God shows his kindness to us while we are yet sinners. In fact, kindness is one way God draws us to himself. I used to think it was God's wrath that caused people to repent. I remember living in a city ravaged by a hurricane. The place was almost devastated. Wreckage and damage were everywhere. I thought such destruction would cause a revival to sweep the city. Not so! It was all about rebellion and hostility. Then I read about the devastation the Bible describes in a future day. Right in the middle of the devastation it says they, "still did not repent . . . nor did they repent" (Rev. 9:20–21). Continue reading in Revelation 16:9–11, "They were seared by the intense heat and they cursed the name of God, who had control over these plagues, but they refused to repent and glorify him. The fifth angel poured out his bowl on the throne of the beast, and his kingdom was plunged into darkness. Men gnawed their tongues in agony and cursed the God of heaven because of their pains and their sores, but they refused to repent of what they had done." Judgment does not seem to bring repentance. Romans 2:4 says, ". . . not realizing that God's kindness leads you toward repentance?"

What breaks our hard, rebellious hearts? His kindness! Maybe you are dealing with a strong-willed child. I'd say your best hope is kindness. Not indulgence, but kindness. I'm not saying let the obstinacy rule. But I'm saying, as he or she becomes worse, you become kinder. Get it? Melt them with kindness. Kindness is powerful stuff!

The greatest display of God's kindness is the gift of his Son, the Lord Jesus Christ. Titus 3:4–5 says, "But when the kindness and love of God our Savior appeared, he saved us, not because of righteous things we had done, but because of his mercy. He saved us through the washing of rebirth and renewal by the Holy Spirit." God's kindness came looking for us. First Corinthians 13:4 says "love is kind." God loved us so much that he sent his

Son to seek us in order to save us. That's kindness! We sing about it in the hymn "At Calvary."

"O the love that drew salvation's plan.

O the love that brought it down to man."

A lady was doing social work among the homeless. She found a hungry man, dirty and destitute. She gave him a good meal. The man thanked her for her kindness. "I wish there were more people in the world like you," the homeless man said.

The lady replied, "There are. Look for them."

The man thought and then answered, "Lady, you came looking for me." That's the gospel. It is not that we came looking for God. We didn't. It is that God, in kindness, sent his Son to come looking for us. I'd say God's kindness is *all that*!

Ephesians 2:7 says, "In order that in the coming ages he might show the incomparable riches of his grace, expressed in his kindness to us in Christ Jesus." It could be that we don't fully understand or appreciate just what his kindness means to us. How can we with our finite minds and limited understanding? Only eternity will fully reveal the scope of his kindness to us. Ephesians 2:7 teaches that in the ages to come his kindness will be on display. Now that's cool! The word *show* means "to point out, to demonstrate, or to display." The greatness of God's kindness in sending Jesus to die for us in our awful sinfulness will bring some heavy-duty amazement to us and to the angels in eternity.

Ever visited a school? Near the entrance there is usually a trophy case. These are the trophies the athletic, academic, and musical teams have won. They point out the victories and achievements of the students of the school. Think about it. We are going to be shining trophies of God's kindness throughout eternity. He will show us off to an amazed universe. Could it be that when an angel wants to understand the kindness of God, the Lord will pick a redeemed saint and display him or her? Any old saint will do. The saint who was once lost, disobedient, depraved, and doomed. God in kindness sent the Lord Jesus to lift him from inevitable death to life, from darkness to light. God saved him and made him like Jesus. All because of his kindness. The halls of heaven and the universities of the universe will shake, rattle, and roll with glory to God in the highest for his kindness. Am I getting carried away with the kindness of God? I'm telling you, God's kindness is *all that*!

The Old Testament saints regularly praised God for his kindness. Psalm 106:1 says, "Praise the LORD. / Give thanks to the LORD, for he is good; / his love endures forever."

"Praise the LORD, all you nations; / extol him, all you peoples. / For great is his love toward us, / and the faithfulness of the LORD endures forever. / Praise the LORD" (Ps. 117:1–2). In the light of a clearer picture of God's kindness since the New Testament and the coming of Christ, should we be even more so constantly amazed and awed by the kindness of God? What is God's appeal to those who do not know him? "Taste and see that the LORD is good" (Ps. 34:8).

One day a little boy was coming home from the store carrying a bucket of honey. As he walked, he dipped his finger in the honey to taste it. A man watched the boy and chuckled. He said, "Son, what's in that bucket?"

"Honey," the boy replied matter-of-factly.

"Is it sweet?" asked the man.

"It sure is," the boy smiled.

"How sweet?" asked the man.

"Very sweet," replied the boy.

"How sweet is very sweet?" the man asked.

"Very, very sweet," said the boy.

"If it is sweet, why can't you tell me how sweet it is?" the man asked.

In exasperation, the boy finally held the bucket of honey out and said, "Here, mister, taste and see for yourself."

That's the Lord's invitation to every person. "Come and experience my kindness. It is sweet to the soul!"

So what makes kindness *all that*?

Expressing Kindness

Once you experience kindness yourself, you will be enabled by the Holy Spirit to express kindness to others. Ephesians 4:32 teaches that we are to be kind to one another. Too many Christians have a hard-edged version of Christianity. I know many people are turned away from the faith by the unkind behavior of legalistic Christians. Convictions are fine, and living a separated, holy life is a desirable goal. But how those convictions are handled is crucial.

Have you ever held a lobster? It's not exactly the softest thing you'll ever hold. Why? Because a lobster has an exoskeleton. Its bone structure is on the outside. Humans have an endoskeleton. Our bone is covered by our flesh. This means we're soft! But the lobster is hard and unappealing because it carries its bones on the outside. Far too many Christians handle their convictions this way. They parade their convictions in a harsh, unloving manner. They show no compassion. No love. No kindness. This world needs kindness. If not from us, then from whom will lost people receive kindness? D. L. Moody said, "We must not be a terror for sinners, but a haven for them."[7]

Do you want some examples? Think about Joseph. He really had a thing for kindness. His own brothers shipped him off to slavery. He then had several years to think about their cruelty to him. Did he become bitter? No. Instead, Joseph was especially kind to his brothers. He showed "undeserved kindness." Joseph's brothers had been cruel, but they didn't get what they deserved. They got kindness.

I guess the best illustration of kindness in the Old Testament involves David and Mephibosheth (see 2 Sam. 9). David certainly didn't have the good life in his early years. He spent thirty years working for a spear-throwing King Saul. He survived this deranged, jealous, hate-filled man. He probably had some pent-up frustration after that job. The day came when it was all over. Saul was dead. Customarily, new kings murdered all the family of the previous regime. But what did David do? He said, "Is there anyone still left of the house of Saul to whom I can show kindness for Jonathan's sake?" (2 Sam. 9:1). How did he do that? Why did he do that? *For Jonathan's sake.* The Old Testament word used here is *hesed.* It carries the idea of a flow of affection or the flow of a mother's milk. David expressed more than human kindness. He showed the kindness of God to the grandson of his enemy Saul.

That's a beautiful picture of God's kindness to a sinner, wouldn't you say? Picture Mephibosheth. In the wrong family. Crippled by a fall. Living in a land without pasture. One day he is called and carried to the feet of David. I bet his heart was pounding. He just knew judgment was going to fall. But instead of judgment, he received kindness from King David. Can you see God's kindness to us in the example? God, in his kindness, seeks, saves, and satisfies us. Mephibosheth was seated at David's table. In the same way, God's kindness seats us at his banquet table. Our kindness to others should be a picture of God's kindness to us. Kindness really is *all that*.

Of course, Jesus is *all that* too! Read the New Testament life of the Lord, and you see his gentleness and kindness everywhere. When Jesus came, his life showed us what God is like. True, God is a God of wrath. But he is also a God of kindness. "Consider therefore the kindness and sternness of God: sternness to those who fell, but kindness to you, provided that you continue in his kindness. Otherwise, you also will be cut off" (Rom. 11:22). Jesus spent his time showing kindness to all kinds of people. Remember the man at the pool of Bethesda? No one was kind to him. They rushed by him, probably with heads down, into the pool. Jesus came and healed him. That's kindness. When he dealt with the woman at the well, we see his kindness. She was very rude and unpleasant. Jesus responded with kindness. Jesus was also kind to little children. The disciples were often irritated by children and wanted to shuffle them off and shut them up. Not Jesus. He took time to be kind to children. James Merritt says, "When Jesus came He poured the milk of human kindness into every bowl of human suffering."

I encourage you to allow the Holy Spirit to help you be kind in your relationships. Kindness is needed at home. Husband and wife relations work better when kindness is a prominent ingredient. When the husband has a listening ear to his wife's frustrations and burdens of the day, he is being kind. When the wife expresses thanks for the unexpected and extra things her husband does for her, she is being kind.

Parents should be kind to their children. I remember my dad's kindness to me on two special occasions. When I was about ten I was throwing a baseball against the brick chimney on the side of our house. Yeah, you guessed it! I threw a little high and broke out a window. Well, let's just say

I didn't want to see my dad right then. Do you know what he did? He just said, "We'll get it fixed." He was so kind. Picture me at seventeen, driving the new family car. Talk about a cream puff. Hard-top convertible. Cream top, sky blue body. I was cookin' with gas! Somehow, I got scraped down the whole side by a black T-model, and I had to pick up my dad! I could just see it. My death, my funeral, you know. My dad looked at it and said, "Well, we can get it fixed." He became my friend for life. His kindness overwhelmed me.

A mother had gotten into the habit of complaining hatefully at home. It all seemed to focus on her little girl. One night, at bedtime prayers, the girl prayed, "Dear God, make Mommy be kind to us like she is to people who visit."

We should apply kindness in our daily activities. Think about your job. There's room for kindness, right? When others are disagreeable and obnoxious in a meeting, we tend to react naturally with hostility and unkindness. But supernatural kindness can ease a tense situation. Kindness can take off the pressure.

A young lady went to work for an executive who had a reputation as being very hard and critical. People didn't work for him long. He was tough. His secretaries lasted only a few months. This young lady began her work by giving him a compliment each day. "That's fine material you have put together for the report," she would say. "What a lovely, attractive suit you are wearing today," she would say. Others in the office noticed that the hard-nosed executive was softening. He eventually became a lovable boss. And, by the way, the new secretary eventually became his wife! Kindness wins. Ladies, try it! It might work for you too!

Christians need to be kind in social settings. Think about waiters. They have a hard time. Hard work for low pay. People can be so unkind to them. Christians have a wonderful opportunity to be good representatives for Jesus Christ by being kind to those who serve them in restaurants. "Kindness takes us off the judgment seat and puts us on the mercy seat."[8]

What about church? Well, I'd say that's one place we really need kindness! Can Christians actually be unkind to one another around church?

You bet! An usher was training a new young man to be an usher. He said, "Remember, young man, we have nothing but good, kind Christians in this church *until you try* to seat someone else in their pew."[9]

Christian leaders should be especially kind. Second Corinthians 6:6 says, "In purity, understanding, patience and kindness; in the Holy Spirit and in sincere love." Kindness is one way we prove ourselves ministers of God. You see, leadership is not a call to haughtiness. It is a call to kindness.

Did you ever study about the Roman emperor Nero? Some say before he ruled Rome, he was known as a kind person. But his newfound authority and power turned him into a tyrant. Nero's the one who burned the tarred bodies of Christians to light his gardens at night. Kind of like the two farmers on a journey who stopped at a small-town railroad station. The ticket agent at the window was rude and uncouth to them. As they walked out one farmer smiled and said to the other, "The smaller the station, the bigger the agent."[10]

Let's talk about how to express kindness. One way we express kindness is through our temperament. Remember, *love is kind*. Kindness is shown in the little things. Respecting others' feelings or helping those in need displays kindness. Sending a card to share sympathy shows kindness. People lose their jobs. Are we kind as we share their concern? Sometimes kindness is just being generous to others, even when it's not deserved. Mark Twain said, "Kindness is a language which the deaf can hear and the blind can read."

If you really think about it, kindness is only tested when we are rubbed the wrong way. Kindness isn't a problem when all goes well. The test comes when all goes wrong. Our job is to remain calm when something is difficult, hard, and unpleasant.

We can express kindness through our language. It is said of the virtuous woman of Proverbs, "faithful instruction is on her tongue" (Prov. 31:26). Drescher says, "Kind words are the music of this world."[11] There is something healing about kindness. Dr. W. Bede McGrath, fellow of the American Psychiatric Association, said, "Ninety percent of all mental illness that comes before me could have been prevented, or could yet be cured, by simple kindness."[12] Christians need to show kindness when dealing with nonbelievers.

All kinds of evangelism are being talked about in the church today. The buzz word is "target evangelism." That's all about picking a specific group to target as an object of our gospel witness. What about "special-event evangelism"? That's using big events to draw unbelievers to hear the gospel. "Visitation evangelism" is all about going into the homes with a positive witness for Christ. I like "sports evangelism," which involves using athletic activities as an evangelistic tool. Hey, how about another buzz word? "Kindness evangelism!" Briscoe says, "None is more winsome nor effective than the loving kindness that reaches out in genuine sympathy to the spiritually forlorn and, regardless of personal cost, generously and unstintingly communicates the reality of Christ."[13]

Is kindness *all that?* Well, it very well could be step one to witnessing. Few things are more effective with those who need the Lord than simple acts of kindness. Unkindness turns people away from the faith in disgust. Kindness wins a hearing for the gospel message, a point for our side. Henry Drummond said, "The greatest thing a man can do for the Heavenly Father is to be kind to some of his children."[14]

Embracing Kindness

It's really all about a choice. Do you want kindness in your life? Do you desire this trait in your personality? If so, then understand that a commandment needs to be obeyed. Ephesians 4:32 states, "Be kind . . . to one another." Think about it. Our nature is to be unkind, right? We're often heartless in our dealings with others. Why then does Paul give kindness as a fruit of the Spirit? His letter to the Galatian Christians explains it all! Were they being kind to one another? Not exactly! They were biting, devouring, and consuming each other, like a pack of wild dogs (see Gal. 5:15). Yeah, they were believers, but they certainly weren't kind.

The command to be kind drives us to the Holy Spirit. We simply cannot produce kindness from within ourselves. So we must ask him to produce his kindness in us. He can help us cultivate the SpiritFruit of kindness in our lives. Kindness is *all that!*

R. E. Lee was president of the now William Lee College after the Civil War. He was known as a very kind man. A new student was meeting with

General Lee upon application to the college. The student asked for a copy of the school's rules and regulations. Lee told him there was none in print. "No rules?" The general told him they had only one rule. What was it? "Our only rule is kindness" (from sermon by James Merritt).

Kindness should be worn like clothing. Colossians 3:12 says, "Therefore, as God's chosen people, holy and dearly loved, clothe yourselves with compassion, kindness, humility, gentleness and patience." Kindness is one of the garments in the wardrobe of a well-dressed Christian. Is it hanging in your closet? OK. I agree. Kindness is easier for some people. "It is farther to Calvary for some than for others. Some people seem to be born with a tender nature."[15] I agree.

So Paul seems to have been fairly mean. I don't think he was what you'd call kind! Certainly his dealings with the man Mark were not as kind as they could have been. When we meet him in heaven, I believe Paul might say, "I should have been kinder." As Paul's writings progress, we see him growing in the grace of kindness. For example, 1 Thessalonians 2:7 says, "But we were gentle among you, like a mother caring for her little children." Here he is. Power-tool Paul comparing himself to a gentle, kind mother! What is up with that? Only the Holy Spirit could do this for a guy like Paul. Hey, only the Holy Spirit can do it for a guy like me. Kindness is *all that*!

Do you have kindness in your closet? Here are some suggestions about how to wear it well. One, take time to be kind. Kindness means time and effort. It's all about making up the mind to be kind. We're so consumed and obsessed with our own interests and activities that we don't take the time to be kind.

Do you remember Lenin and Russian history? Lenin wrapped himself so completely in the words he wrote to start the revolution that he lost all capacity to be gentle and kind. He became a miserable person. He made people around him miserable also, mainly his wife. One night his wife, exhausted, left her sick mother's bedside to seek some rest. She asked Lenin, who was working and writing at the table, to wake her if her mother needed her. The next morning she awoke to find her mother dead. Lenin was still writing at the table. Brokenhearted, she asked him why he did not come for her. "You told me to wake you if your mother needed you. She died. She didn't need you."[16] Don't get so wrapped up in a job, a hobby, or a sport that you don't see opportunities for kindness.

Jesus always had time to be kind. I mention the little children again. Nobody was ever busier or had a more important assignment than Jesus. Yet along the way he stopped. He took the time to bless the little children. He was kind to the woman at the well. He took time to fill her thirsty soul with the water of life. He saw others and their needs. He looked outward, not constantly inward, as we seem to do in our culture today.

Take time to be kind. And try to be kind all the time. I know it's hard, nerves on the edge. Tension in the muscles. Harsh words are on our lips. That's when we need to ask the Holy Spirit to help us to put on kindness.

What is the SpiritFruit of kindness about? Well, just like the rest of the fruit, its purpose is to make us like Jesus. As we become kinder, we become more like Jesus. Leonardo da Vinci was working on his *Last Supper*. In the course of its painting, he became angry and lost his temper with a friend. He lashed out with bitter words. Returning to his canvas, he attempted to work on the face of Jesus. But he couldn't. No matter how he tried, he just couldn't paint the face of Jesus. So he put down his tools, sought out the man, and asked for forgiveness. The man accepted his apology. Leonardo then returned and finished the face of Jesus. The fact is, people will see Jesus in us when they see kindness in us.

Can you say *revival*? Do you think we need one? I do! What kind of revival do we need? Of the spectacular? Not necessarily. Of kindness? Amen!

Did you know that the Greek word for *Christ* and the Greek word for *kind* are quite similar. The word for kindness is *chrestos*. The Greek word for Christ is *christos*. One letter. That's it!

It is said that in the early years of the Christian faith, pagans confused these words for kindness and Christ. They couldn't decide if Christianity was a religion based on someone named Christos or a religion based on Chrestos, kindness.[17] If only people today coming into daily contact with Christians could be so confused! Yes, kindness is *all that* and more!

CHAPTER 8

THE GRAPES OF GOODNESS

"And in the eyes of the people there is a failure; and in the eyes of the hungry there is a growing wrath. In the souls of the people the grapes of wrath are filling and growing heavy, growing heavy for the vintage."[1]

This excerpt comes from John Steinbeck's classic *The Grapes of Wrath*. This novel won a Pulitzer Prize in 1940 and was later made into a motion picture starring Henry Fonda. Steinbeck tells his readers of the hard lives lived by the Joad family. The Joads move from Oklahoma to California in search of work as migrant fruit pickers. They experience many hardships, symbolically represented as the grapes of wrath, yet in the end, the human spirit endures.

The reference to these grapes of wrath is actually taken from the Bible. In fact, grapes are often used symbolically in the Bible. For example, Israel's sin is compared to wild grapes in Isaiah 5:2. The sins of a rebellious world are judged in "the great winepress of God's wrath" in Revelation 14:18–20. Crushed grapes are actually an image of divine judgment.[2]

Yet grapes are also used in a positive way in the Bible. Grapes often symbolize abundance and prosperity. One of my favorite office knick-knacks is a wood carving of a gigantic cluster of grapes held by two of the twelve spies who surveyed the promised land for Israel. The large grapes in the carving symbolize the fertility and productivity of the land described in Numbers 13:23. Grapes also symbolize the divine blessing in the age to come when the crops will be so bountiful that one crop will be on top of another (Amos 9:13).

So what's up with grapes? What is their relevance to the fruit of the Spirit? Grapes are cultivated on all continents and islands with a suitable climate. I was surprised to learn that there are between six thousand and eight thousand varieties of grapes. Only forty to sixty of these varieties are commercially important. Grapes come in many colors and sizes. I like the Concord grape. This large blue-black, almost purple, fruit is tough-skinned but very flavor-filled. I guess the Thompson seedless is my favorite. It is the most common. Light green and medium-sized, its sweet, juicy meat makes the tart skin worth the bite!

Grapes constitute the largest fruit industry on the globe. Sometimes they are dried into raisins or crushed for juice or canned for jelly and fruit cocktail. They are used in salads, desserts, and pies. Soft, sweet, bite-sized grapes are delicious when they are fresh. Eaten alone they provide a very enjoyable, low-calorie snack. In reality, grapes are sometimes called "The Queen of Fruits" because they possess excellent cleansing properties for the human body. Grapes detoxify the body and help build iron-rich blood.[3] So eat more grapes!

When I read that the fruit of the Spirit is goodness, I think about the grapes. The grapes of goodness. Why? Because there is nothing more effective than God's goodness to remove spiritual and secular poisons or toxins from the human soul. There is nothing better than Spirit-produced goodness to bring health and cleansing to every relationship in our lives.

The particular word used for goodness is found only three other times in the New Testament. In a similar statement, Ephesians 5:9 says, "For the fruit of the light consists in all goodness, righteousness and truth." The other two times are in Romans 15:14 and 2 Thessalonians 1:11. We will look at these in a moment.

Goodness is not easy to define. *Agathos* is translated "good," meaning that which is excellent in any sphere of life. It is used to describe a gift (Matt. 7:11), a person (Matt. 12:35), a tree (Matt. 7:17–18), a slave (Matt. 25:21), fertile ground (Luke 8:8), conscience (Acts 23:1), the will of God (Rom. 12:2), Christian hope (2 Thess. 2:16), and Christian works (Eph. 2:10).[4] Goodness comes from the same word family as the word *good*.

Thayer defines goodness as "uprightness of heart and life."[5] Barclay says that goodness is "virtue equipped at every point." It is doing good for others in a practical way. Galatians 6:10 urges, "Therefore, as we have opportunity, let us do good to all people, especially to those who belong to the family of believers." Yes, we all have opportunities, don't we? A. Z. Conrad calls goodness "an abandoned waif-neglected, abused, misunderstood. Of royal blood, yet snubbed, sneered at and avoided. Highest and holiest in the category of virtues, yet disowned and undesired."[6] What do you think about that? Drescher adds a helpful statement about goodness. "Goodness deals primarily with the *motives* of our speech and conduct. It lies at the heart of our character, behind all we say and do."[7] You know, the Anglo-Saxon word *God* meant "good" in that language. Good and God, as we shall see, are related. Leave God out of good and only zero is left!

Goodness means a lot of things to a lot of people. For some, it's all about pleasure. The idea is, if I experience pleasure, then it is good. If I experience pain, then it is bad. This idea of goodness has some serious consequences: if you experience pain in marriage, that's bad, so for your good, get out; you owe it to yourself!

For others goodness is knowledge. The idea is if people know good they will do it. Yeah, right! It just doesn't work that way! So does knowing what's good guarantee that people will do it? No way! Roger knows he should study for his chemistry exam, but he meets his friends at the movies instead. An uneducated thief quietly boards a railroad car in the middle of the night. He steals a melon and rushes from the car. An educated thief walks into the corporate boardroom and steals the train!

What exactly is goodness? Some say it is the greatest benefit for the greatest number of people. Hold up! This idea creates some major problems. How can someone accurately judge what is the greatest benefit for all?

For others, goodness is having things. I think we all know that temptation! Wealth is viewed as being synonymous with goodness. Sears is even running ads about "giving the good life." What is the "good life"? A nice car, an elaborate house, a trophy wife, and plenty of money to spend? But wait, this doesn't compute either. Having many things is often a curse.

Some Christians equate goodness with not doing some things. This is a negative goodness, also called legalism. People are good, according to legalism, if they don't do certain things. You know the old song, "I don't smoke, and I don't chew, and I don't go with girls that do. Our team won a Bible." Fruit of the Spirit goodness? I don't think so!

A study of goodness in the Bible shows us it is a God-like trait. We are told that God the Father is a God of goodness. Romans 11:22 says, "Consider therefore the kindness and sternness of God: sternness to those who fell, but kindness to you, provided that you continue in his kindness. Otherwise, you also will be cut off." God is good in his person. "With praise and thanksgiving they sang to the LORD: 'He is good; his love to Israel endures forever'" (Ezra 3:11). "For the LORD is good and his love endures forever; / his faithfulness continues through all generations" (Ps. 100:5). "The LORD is good, a refuge in times of trouble. He cares for those who trust in him" (Nah. 1:7).

We see the goodness of God in his precepts or laws. "The grass withers and the flowers fall, but the word of our God stands forever" (Isa. 40:8). God's Word is good. What he says is good. What he teaches is good. What he commands is good. What he promises is good.

We see God's goodness in his purposes. Because God is good, what he does is good. Read again the creation account. All along the way we are told that God saw it was good. Then, at the end, God calls it all *very good* (Gen. 1:31).

Romans 8:28 reminds us that God is working all things for our good. But this does not mean all things are good. It means that God has a purpose for everything he allows to come our way. Whatever the personal circumstances or situations, God promises they will ultimately be for our good.

God gives good things. "Every good and perfect gift is from above, coming down from the Father of the heavenly lights, who does not change like shifting shadows" (James 1:17). "The LORD will indeed give what is good, and our land will yield its harvest" (Ps. 85:12). He gives us his will for our lives, and that is good. "Do not conform any longer to the pattern of this world, but be transformed by the renewing of your mind. Then you will be able to test and approve what God's will is—his good, pleasing and perfect will" (Rom. 12:2).

Do you remember the rich young ruler who came to Jesus? He came paying Jesus a compliment, "good teacher . . ." (Mark 10:17). Jesus responded in a strange way. "Why do you call me good? No one is good—except God alone" (Mark 10:18). It was like a pan of cold water in the ruler's face. Why did Jesus respond that way? Basically, he wanted the young man to search his soul. He was saying to him—there are only two possibilities, "If you want to call me good, you must call me God. If you won't call me God, you can't call me good." Jesus demonstrated his deity by his goodness and left the rich young ruler with a choice.

Perhaps goodness was the most outstanding characteristic humans saw of the Lord. Acts 10:38 tells us, "How God anointed Jesus of Nazareth with the Holy Spirit and power, and how he went around doing good and healing all who were under the power of the devil, because God was with him." Interesting connection! Jesus was anointed by the Spirit, and the result was that he went about doing good. Would this be evidence of the anointing of the Spirit? Yes! How did Jesus demonstrate his anointing of the Spirit? He went around doing good. So what about people being anointed by the Spirit today? The greatest evidence of anointing is that their lives are filled with the grapes of goodness. If you were looking for Jesus in Bible days, how would you find him? You'd look for a person helping others. How would you find a Spirit-filled Christian today? By finding Christians helping others.

The Bible also tells about the goodness of the Holy Spirit. "Teach me to do your will, for you are my God; / may your good Spirit lead me on level ground" (Ps. 143:10). "You gave your good spirit to instruct them. You did not withhold your manna from their mouths, and you gave them water for their thirst" (Neh. 9:20). The aim of the Holy Spirit is to produce good people. This is why we are told that the fruit of the Spirit is in *all* goodness in Ephesians 5:9. The word *all* is added to underscore the value of goodness and the Spirit's purpose to produce that goodness in our lives.

People have potential to do great good or great evil. Perhaps you remember reading Robert Louis Stevenson's *Dr. Jekyll and Mr. Hyde*. Actually, all of us find a Jekyll and Hyde in ourselves, don't we? Paul discusses this yin-and-yang battle between the good and the evil in us. In Romans 7:21 he declares, "So I find this law at work: When I want to do good, evil is right there with me." We desire to do good, but evil is all mixed in.

Human capacity to do evil is shocking. We read of the Holocaust. Some of the Nazi scientific experiments stun us. Little children were infected with germs, and the scientists watched them die. Furnaces were built to burn millions of people. Ignorance? Half of Hitler's high command had master's and doctor's degrees. They showed us how evil men can be to their fellow men.

Romans 12:21 urges us, "Do not be overcome by evil, but overcome evil with good." Just how do we do this? It is interesting to me that the human struggle between good and evil that Paul portrays in Romans 7 is followed by the magnificent Romans 8 passage. It details the work of the Holy Spirit in the life of the believer. We can overcome our evil human nature and do good only as the Holy Spirit produces the grapes of goodness in our lives.

This goodness is not exactly a natural trait of human personality. While human beings do demonstrate various degrees of goodness, we are not naturally good. Goodness is all about the Holy Spirit, and the Spirit must produce it in us. Goodness is not natural. It is supernatural. Remember the nursery rhyme about the little girl with the curl? It goes like this:

There was a little girl
With a little curl
Right in the middle of her forehead.
When she was good
She was very, very good.
When she was bad, she was horrid.

That describes all of us, doesn't it?

Let's look at the other two verses that use the word *goodness*, Romans 15:14 and 2 Thessalonians 1:11. These two verses talk to us specifically about being good and doing good.

Step One: Being Good
How to be Filled Full of Goodness

The King James Version renders Romans 15:14, "And I myself also am persuaded of you, my brethren, that ye also are *full of goodness*, filled with all knowledge, able also to admonish one another." Being good comes before doing good. Paul is telling us that it is actually possible for us to be full of goodness. It's an amazing truth. We know God is good, and we know that we are not good! "All have turned away, they have together become worthless; there is no one who does good, not even one" (Rom. 3:12). "I know that nothing good lives in me, that is, in my sinful nature. For I have the desire to do what is good, but I cannot carry it out" (Rom. 7:18).

When Adam and Eve fell in the garden of Eden, we all fell. The tragedy of Eden is the universal human tragedy. Adam and Eve were allowed to eat the fruit from all of the trees of the garden except one—the tree of the knowledge of good and evil. Good in Eden was defined by doing God's will and obeying his word. Evil was disobeying his word and not doing his will. We know the sad story. Adam and Eve made a choice to eat the forbidden fruit; and when they did, sin entered humanity and mankind fell. They received the knowledge of good and evil all right. They knew evil but were powerless to avoid it. They knew good and were powerless to do it. Today, we know good and evil, but we're just not always able to do the one and avoid the other.

We've discussed that goodness is not something acquired naturally. It is inconsistent with our fallen, sinful nature. We cannot manufacture goodness. Too often, we have the idea that people are basically good. To be honest, I operated on that false premise for many years. I assumed everyone would be truthful to me. I bought a lot of bad merchandise that way! I was actually operating unbiblically. People are basically bad. Yeah, you're right. That's a pessimistic view of people. But it is the Bible view! Romans 7:18 (KJV) says, *in me . . . no good thing.*

Goodness can only come from God. Remember the rich young ruler who came to Jesus? Jesus talked to him about the Ten Commandments. It seems the rich young ruler had a very shallow idea of goodness. His response when Jesus brought up the commandments was, "Teacher, all these I have kept since I was a boy" (Mark 10:20). OK, that was probably true. He probably had lived a nice life. But Jesus was trying to get him to probe deeper. Like so many today, the ruler cast a careless glance at his life, being satisfied with a shallow goodness and external respectability. He pronounced himself good. Jesus wanted him to look deeper. He wanted him to see the inner nature of the law or his consciousness. It is by the law that we have knowledge of sin. This law acts as a mirror, showing us our true selves. Human goodness apart from Jesus Christ is the worst form of badness. It is a deceptive, surface-level goodness, and it is comforting to our view of ourselves. Such shallow goodness can lull a person right into hell. The truth is—if we look at ourselves closely in the mirror of the law—we will see all of our badness in living color!

So there is only one way to be truly good. It's called the goodness of God. And we can get it only by a new birth experience. When we receive Christ as Savior, we become born again. This means we share in God's divine nature. Second Peter 1:4 says, ". . . so that through them you may participate in the divine nature . . ." This is the only way we can be truly good.

Becoming full of goodness can happen only through the Holy Spirit.

Yes, goodness is all about a change of heart brought about by the Holy Spirit. The words of Jesus help us here. He said, "The good man brings good things out of the good stored up in him, and the evil man brings evil things out of the evil stored up in him" (Matt. 12:35).

Goodness is not just about the good things you do. It is also about the fruit the Holy Spirit produces in and through your life. That's why the Bible says the fruit of the Spirit is goodness. It is not human goodness. No way! It is the goodness of God brought about by the Holy Spirit.

Think about this! How do we know people are filled with the Spirit? Perhaps because they are good? Barnabas is one of my favorite New Testament personalities. He was an encourager. Acts 11:24 tells us all about him: "He was a good man, full of the Holy Spirit and faith, and a great number of people were brought to the Lord." Notice the connection between goodness and being filled with the Holy Spirit. In fact, his goodness is mentioned before his fullness! How will people know we are Spirit-filled? Maybe they will see it in our goodness.

Step Two: Doing Good
How to Fulfill Goodness

Let's look at 2 Thessalonians 1:11. The phrase is *fulfill . . . goodness*. Being good is what we are on the inside. Doing good is what people see on the outside. It's not just a kindly disposition—it's also kindly action. One of the best definitions of goodness I have read is that goodness is "personal godliness lived out in a practical way."

Note that it is *his* goodness, not *our* goodness, that we are to fulfill. Mankind cannot do good on its own. It's God's goodness we should show in our daily lives.

One lady excitedly shared with her friend, "Our weight loss club has had great success. We've lost 148 lbs. However, none of it is mine personally." The same can be said for Holy Spirit goodness that is not produced by us personally. The Holy Spirit is given to help us be good and do good. There are several ways we can do good and so fulfill his goodness in our lives.

One way we fulfill goodness is doing good in our walk with Christ. Think about Ephesians 5:9 and its context. The verses before and after talk about our daily walk or lifestyle. Basically, this passage is a New Testament picture of Psalm 37:23, "If the LORD delights in a man's way, he makes his steps firm." In other words, we are to do good in our daily lives. As we live in relationship with other people, which we all have, we are simply to do good.

Well, just how do we determine what is good? By what we think is good? Not exactly! Today, we deal with the same mentality that people did during the biblical period of the judges. In that day, "everyone did as he saw fit" (Judg. 17:6). But what we think is good is not always best. Proverbs 14:12 says, "There is a way that seems right to a man, but in the end it leads to death."

What about our feelings? Do we determine what is good by how we feel about it? Some do. The tragic death of John F. Kennedy Jr. could have been avoided. Many experts believe he suffered from vertigo before the crash. His feelings told him one thing. The controls may have told him another. Too often we want to take things in our own hands and go by our feelings. But goodness is not determined by our feelings.

What about the crowd? Do we determine the good by a majority vote? "Everybody's doing it." That's a shabby rationale for behavior. The fact that everybody is doing something does not make it good. Use of alcohol, drugs, promiscuous sex—are they all determined by majority vote? No way! There must be a better basis for determining goodness, and there is. Everybody is *not* doing it!

There is only one basis for determining goodness, and that is the teaching of God's Word. The Word of the Lord shows us the way to goodness.

One way to fulfill God's goodness is by doing good work. Psalm 37:3 urges, "Trust in the LORD and do good; dwell in the land and enjoy safe pasture." "Command them to do good, to be rich in good deeds, and to be generous and willing to share" (1 Tim. 6:18). We are not saved by our good works, but we are saved unto good works. This is the progression explained in Ephesians 2:8–10. Let's emphasize some words for you. "By grace—through faith—unto good works." See it? There is a distinct progression. Our good works don't save us, but because we are saved, we should do good works.

The Old Testament prophet Micah is one who showed us the way to goodness. He said, "He has showed you, O man, what is good. And what does the LORD require of you? To act justly and to love mercy and to walk humbly with your God" (Mic. 6:8). This means we are to do good to all people. "Therefore, as we have opportunity, let us do good to all people, especially to those who belong to the family of believers" (Gal. 6:10).

Another good definition of *goodness* is "love in action." Simply acting out our love in practical, helpful ways defines goodness. Goodness is reading the Bible to an elderly person in the rest home. Goodness is explaining God's simple way of salvation to the derelict in a jail cell. Goodness is taking a meal to a mom whose child has been sick for days on end. "To do good is to see no duty too small to do, and to see no task too meager to tackle, to see no person too insignificant to encourage and lift, and to see no person too unimportant to help, to see no feet too unclean to stoop and wash."[8]

The Bible gives some beautiful illustrations of fulfilling goodness. One of my favorites is the story of Dorcas. We read about her in Acts 9. Dorcas was not a preacher. She had no spectacular sign gifts of the New Testament era. You may remember, Dorcas was the woman Simon Peter raised from the dead. We are told that she was *full of good works and almsdeeds which she did*. What does that mean? Verse 39 tells that all the widows stood around her dead body as Peter entered the room and they showed him the coats and garments Dorcas had made them while she was with them. Dorcas did good deeds with her needle. She had a gift to sew. She used her gift to do good things for people. What Dorcas was on the inside was demonstrated by her loving sewing on the outside. The good works on the outside are proof of the goodness of God on the inside.

Fulfilling goodness is also doing good in our witness. First Peter 2:12 is an interesting verse. It talks about those who "accuse you of doing wrong." Even the early church had its critics. Surprise, surprise! They were slandered. They were falsely accused of cannibalism, of immorality, and of subverting the government. We have the same kinds of criticisms and attacks today, don't we? How should they be handled? "They may see your good deeds and glorify God on the day he visits us" (1 Pet. 2:12). The best answer to the critics is a lovely Christlike life. In other words, live in such a way that no one will believe the accusations against you. The verse continues that these good works seen by people may *glorify God in the day of visitation*. Maybe this means when a crisis or disaster comes, people will come to the Christian, whose good works they have seen, for help. The lovely life of a Christian and the good works that life produces may help win lost people. Jesus put it this way: "Let your light shine before men, that they may see your good deeds and praise your Father in heaven" (Matt. 5:16).

The consistent life of a Christian is a powerful evangelistic force. Because of Barnabas's good works, "a great number of people were brought to the Lord" (Acts 11:24). Second Thessalonians 1:11, which talks about fulfilling goodness, continues in verse 12 by saying, "that the name of our Lord Jesus may be glorified in you." What's that all about? Our good works provide a powerful witness to the reality of the Christian faith.

"You are writing a Gospel,
    a chapter each day.
By deeds that you do,
    by words that you say.
Men see what you write,
    whether you're faithless or true.
Say what is the Gospel According to You?"

All of us face the struggle of the two natures. We want to do good, but evil is always there. Romans 12:21 tells us we are to overcome this evil by doing good. Again, we are faced with the tension between the fruit of the Spirit as a command and the fruit of the Spirit as produced by the Holy Spirit. How do we solve the tension? We yield to the Holy Spirit, confessing our failure to obey the command. Then, having yielded to him, he produces God's goodness in and through us.

Romans 12:9 says, ". . . Hate what is evil; cling to what is good." The word *cling* means "to glue or cement together." We are to glue ourselves to the good. Stick to the good. Peterson puts it this way, "Hold on for dear life to good." As we seek the good in the power of the Holy Spirit, our lives will produce not the grapes of wrath, but the grapes of goodness for ourselves and for others.

CHAPTER 9

A-PEELING
FAITHFULNESS

Buying bananas is part of my Saturday routine. I buy lots of bananas! I call the banana "my old reliable." I find peeling a banana an appealing experience. Let's just say I depend on a good banana to satisfy my sweet craving and to provide a quick surge of energy. To me, the banana is the most reliable fruit of all.

Most of us enjoy yellow bananas. Although there are other varieties, the yellow banana is the most commonly seen and eaten in the U.S. Yellow bananas appeared in 1836. A Jamaican, Jean Francois Poujot, observed one morning some uniquely yellow fruit on his plantation trees. Upon tasting this strange new fruit, he found them very edible uncooked. When ripe they were sweet and delicious. Poujot immediately saw the potential and began to plant banana trees. We know the result. The yellow banana has become one of the most popular fresh fruits in America.

Bananas are enjoyable in many ways. Of course, they can be eaten raw, once peeled out of their jackets. Bananas are delicious in all kinds of things. Banana ice cream! Um, um! Bananas in cakes! My, my. Banana cream pie! Oh, boy. Banana bread! Delicious, delicious. And my most favorite of all, banana pudding! Yabba-dabba-do!

Why do I think this yellow fruit is so reliable? Bananas can be very faithful to your health needs. Bananas are basically a powerhouse of nutritional energy. They contain a great deal of fiber. They're loaded with vitamins and minerals, and they are especially high in potassium. One average size banana has almost four milligrams of potassium. Distance runners find that bananas help replenish diminishing levels of potassium. Bananas benefit the muscular and nervous systems. Their sugar can be readily assimilated as body fuel.

Bananas contain pectin, which helps heal ulcers and lower blood cholesterol. Bananas are also rich in an amino acid, tryptophan, which is known to promote sleep (maybe that's why I get sleepy so early at night!).[1] The banana will indeed be faithful to your system. You can always depend on it. The banana—an old reliable!

The Bible says the fruit of the Spirit is faithfulness. This is the seventh fruit of the Spirit mentioned in Galatians 5:22–23. I believe *faithfulness* is the best word to translate the meaning. The word *faith* is actually used in three different ways in Galatians. Galatians 1:23 talks about "the faith," referring to the substance or content of the Christian gospel. Galatians 3:14

talks about faith for salvation. This is the faith we exercise in trusting Christ as our personal Savior. Then, in Galatians 5:22, faith means faithfulness. Not faith in the sense of belief in God or in the substance of Christian doctrine, but the faithful doing of our Christian duties unto the Lord and others. Of course, faith should produce faithfulness. In a sense, faith is the root and faithfulness is the fruit. Get the picture? Used in the context of the fruit of the Spirit, faithfulness is that trait of Christian character produced by the Holy Spirit's enabling us to be reliable and dependable.

Faithfulness is greatly appreciated and desired today, isn't it? Even in secular life. Have you ever been to a fiftieth wedding anniversary? Guests congratulate the couple on their perseverance and the longevity of their marriage. They hold hands like teenage lovers. They embrace and publicly thank one another for their faithfulness.

A smiling gray-haired lady was attending her retirement banquet after forty years of service to the company. The CEO presented her with a gold watch, a generous pension check, and thanked her for her faithfulness. Is faithfulness desired? You bet! But it's rare today, isn't it? Too few companies show much faithfulness toward their workers. Companies are often sold out from under the workers. Next thing you hear, the top execs move to Maui with their millions. For the same reason, many workers jump from one job to another for a few hundred dollars extra. It seems that for Generation X the only commitment is to personal happiness. Faithfulness is desired and appreciated. There just seems to be a short supply of it today. That's why faithfulness is so appealing.

The fruit of the Spirit is faithfulness. The word here was used commonly in secular Greek for the idea of trustworthiness. It is the characteristic of a person who is reliable. This sort of person is called faithful.[2] As used in this context, faithfulness is being dependable in the discharge of our duties and in our devotion to people and principles.[3] Peterson says that faithfulness is "the freedom to be involved in long-term loyal commitments based on invisible values and meanings rather than immediate and tangible self-interest."[4] James Merritt gives the most concise definition of faithfulness I have ever read. He says, "Faithfulness is doing your duty until your duty is done"!

God also places a high premium on faithfulness. That pretty much settles it! We are told that Moses was "faithful as a servant in all God's house" (Heb. 3:5). The Lord Jesus was faithful to the heavenly Father. "He was faithful to the one who appointed him" (Heb. 3:2).

On the day of Pentecost an astonishing transformation took place in the disciples. Just a few days before, they had been completely faithless to Jesus. Though claiming loyalty to him and vowing to go with him to death, most of them bailed out on him and fled. They left him to die alone. But then, something supernatural happened! On the day of Pentecost they were filled with the Holy Spirit. Suddenly these men who had been faithless became absolutely faithful to the Lord Jesus. During the worst suffering and in the most difficult circumstances, they were faithful to Jesus. What made the difference? The Holy Spirit was producing the grace of faithfulness in and through them.

Faith is presented in 1 Corinthians 12:9 as a spiritual gift. What does it do? It makes power possible. What sort of power? The faith to trust God to do great things in his name. What would you say is hard evidence of a Spirit-filled Christian? The ability to do miracles? Sensational preaching? How about dependability? How about being reliable? Faithfulness is that dependability the Holy Spirit produces in our lives when we are yielded to his control.

William Carey, after eight years as a missionary in India, saw few visible results. A less committed person might have tuned out, but William Carey stayed on the job. He wrote to a friend, "Pray for us that we may be faithful to the end."[5] Certainly the desire of every Christian is to hear the Lord say, "Well done, good and faithful servant! You have been faithful with a few things; I will put you in charge of many things . . ." (Matt. 25:21).

Let's peel and eat this SpiritFruit of faithfulness to see why it is so appealing.

God Exemplifies Faithfulness

We learn from the Bible and in our personal experience with God that he is utterly faithful. We can stake our life and our eternity on his faithfulness. The Bible says, "God is faithful" many times. It seems to me that faithful is the adjective that characteristically describes God. Think about these statements in the Bible: "Let us hold unswervingly to the hope we profess, for he who promised is faithful" (Heb. 10:23). "By faith Abraham, even though he was past age—and Sarah herself was barren—was able to become a father because he considered him faithful who had made the promise" (Heb. 11:11). "Know therefore that the LORD your God is God; he is the faithful God, keeping his covenant of love to a thousand generations of those who love him and keep his commands" (Deut. 7:9). ". . . because of the LORD, who is faithful, the Holy One of Israel, who has chosen you" (Isa. 49:7).

We are also told that God's word is faithful. "All your commands are trustworthy . . ." (Ps. 119:86). This means that the promises of God are completely trustworthy because they are based upon the character of God, who is utterly reliable. The faithfulness of God is really beyond our comprehension. "Great is your faithfulness" (Lam. 3:23). All through the Bible the same message is so appealing especially in this day of disappointment and fear: "You can depend on God."

How is God faithful? God is faithful in his calling. "God, who has called you into fellowship with his Son Jesus Christ our Lord, is faithful" (1 Cor. 1:9). The God who has called us to fellowship with his Son through the new birth experience has committed to be faithful to us. The first verse I memorized after my call to preach the gospel was, "There hath no temptation taken you but such as is common to man: but God is faithful, who will not suffer you to be tempted above that ye are able; but will with the temptation also make a way to escape, that ye may be able to bear it" (1 Cor. 10:13 KJV). God will be faithful to us even in those moments of temptation. You can count on God to provide an escape valve when the temptations come your way. First Peter 4:19 tells us that God is a "faithful Creator." God has created a universe that is dependable and reliable. Do you ever go to bed at night fearing that the sun will not come up in the morning? I don't think so! It will come up right on schedule. We do not have to worry while we exhale about whether there will be any air to inhale. God is faithful. God is a faithful creator.

What about those times when we sin big and need major forgiveness and cleansing? Can we depend on God in those situations? You bet! "If we confess our sins, he is faithful and just and will forgive us our sins, and purify us from all unrighteousness" (1 John 1:9).

The deal is that God remains constant despite our fickleness and our faithlessness. "If we are faithless, he will remain faithful . . ." (2 Tim. 2:13).

The great example of faithfulness in the Bible is the Lord Jesus Christ. He is called in Hebrews 2:17 "a merciful and faithful high priest." This means that Jesus is always there. We can always count on him.

We see the faithfulness of the Lord displayed when he walked on the earth. Think of all Jesus experienced when he was here, yet he never hesitated or faltered. He was utterly trustworthy. He went through fierce temptations from Satan. He was let down by friends and misunderstood by family. He endured sorrow, affliction, hunger, and weariness. Did he become despondent and depressed? No. Through it all Jesus was utterly faithful. He went on doing his Father's business. He went to Gethsemane, where he prayed with great anguish and many tears, "thy will be done." Then, he went on to the cross. There his faithfulness was on splendid display. Revelation 1:5, 3:14, and 19:11 call him "the faithful witness." This means you can stake your life and your eternity on Jesus.

During World War II the king and queen of England were faithful to their subjects. They shared the same inconveniences and losses as private citizens. They waited their turn like everyone else. They endured the same rations and water limits. No wonder they are still so loved by the English people. But such monumental human faithfulness pales in comparison to the faithfulness Jesus shows to us. God is faithful. Jesus is faithful. God exemplifies faithfulness. That's why unpeeling faithfulness is so appealing!

God Expects Faithfulness

God is faithful to us, so he expects us to be faithful. Faithfulness is an essential ingredient in our service to the Lord and in our relationships with other people. "Now it is required that those who have been given a trust must prove faithful" (1 Cor. 4:2). How about the word *required*? Who is requiring? God is. He expects faithfulness. James Merritt tells of the two hundred geysers at Yellowstone National Park. One geyser is the favorite. Do you know which one? No, not the biggest one that shoots water the highest. It is the one called Old Faithful, the really dependable one. Every sixty-five minutes Old Faithful shoots a stream of boiling water 170 feet into the air. This is the crowd's favorite. Tourists gather on the minute to watch it! Just like Old Faithful, you can always depend on the Lord. He's faithful, too. Can the Lord always depend on you?

Think about the New Testament. What did Timothy, Tychicus, Epaphras, Onesimus, Silvanus, and Gaius have in common? Their faithfulness, of course! They are praised for their faithfulness (1 Cor. 4:17; Eph. 6:21; Col. 1:7; 4:9; 1 Pet. 5:12; 3 John 5).

The Holy Spirit is in our lives to make our own character like the character of Jesus. Do you remember Matthew? He was a crooked tax collector. He was an outcast in Jewish society, looked down upon because of his questionable ethics. But Jesus changed him. Jesus called him to be his follower. The Holy Spirit took control of Matthew's life. The result? He wrote the first Gospel. Simon Peter was a rugged fisherman known to use some profane language. Jesus called him to be a fisher of men with him. The Holy Spirit then filled him. What happened? He became a faithful preacher of the gospel. That's what it's all about. That's what the Holy Spirit does in a life. He produces the fruit of faithfulness.

Jesus taught faithfulness in parables. Do you remember the story Jesus told about the steward who had wasted his master's goods? That parable shows the importance of faithfulness. When Jesus came to the climax of the story he said, "Whoever can be trusted with very little can also be trusted with much" (Luke 16:10a).

Whatever our work is, we should be faithful to the Lord in that work. "Whatever your hand finds to do, do it with all your might, for in the grave, where you are going, there is neither working nor planning nor knowledge nor wisdom" (Eccl. 9:10). We often fail to see our secular work as an opportunity to show faithfulness to the Lord. In our workplace we can demonstrate our utter reliability and dependability on him. "Whatever you do, work at it with all your heart, as working for the Lord, not for men" (Col. 3:23).

Let's go back to that parable from Luke 16. Jesus is teaching faithfulness in the use of our material possessions. His point is, faithfulness in our worldly wealth qualifies us for opportunities to be faithful stewards in the true riches or our spiritual wealth (see Luke 16:11–12).

We need to be faithful in worshiping the Lord. Hebrews 10:25 is really needed in these lax, uncommitted days. "Let us not give up meeting together, as some are in the habit of doing, but let us encourage one another—and all the more as you see the Day approaching."

I am privileged to be pastor of some of the finest Christian people I have ever known. I could spend the rest of this book writing about the positive characteristics of our people at First Baptist Church, Jacksonville, Florida. But these churchgoers' most notable trait is their faithfulness to our services. A high percentage of our people attend all the services faithfully. They understand that God expects it.

Hugh Latimer, who was martyred in Oxford for his faith, was a great preacher. As he was preparing to preach for a Sunday service, a voice came to him saying, "Latimer, be careful what you preach today. You are going to preach before the king of England." Then another voice came to him, "Latimer, be careful what you preach today. You are going to preach before the King of kings." When we worship, we come into the presence of the King of kings. How sad that Jesus waits for many of his people to come before him in worship, but they seldom come.

Faithfulness also involves being reliable and dependable in our relationships with others. Do other people find us faithful? If you think about it, you realize that every area of life provides opportunities to be faithful.

Faithfulness is so important that a society doesn't function well without it. It takes a lot of faithful service for life as we know it to function properly. We count upon our pharmacist to be faithful to fill the correct prescriptions. We depend on the pilot to be faithful to navigate the plane by the proper guidelines. Definitely! We rely on the cook in our favorite restaurant to serve clean, cooked food. Amen!

Can you think of a human characteristic more disappointing than unfaithfulness? "Like a bad tooth or a lame foot is reliance on the unfaithful in times of trouble" (Prov. 25:19). Faithfulness is rare. "Many a man claims to have unfailing love, but a faithful man who can find?" (Prov. 20:6).

We should be faithful to our families. Husband and wife should be faithful to each other. Moms and dads, sons and daughters, should be faithful to each other. This dependability and reliability makes the home function better. Teaching faithfulness in the home prepares family members to relate better to the world around them. We need to be faithful to our promises and our commitments, don't we? Whatever our duty, we need to do it and do it faithfully. Can people count on you?

Two young men were bosom buddies during World War II. One day the battle was fierce, and one friend was struck by a bullet while their regiment retreated. Jim pleaded with his commanding officer for permission to return to the battle and to bring back his buddy. At first, the commander was reluctant. Because of Jim's persistence, the commander finally allowed him to return to the field. Jim found his friend near death. Jim put him on his shoulders and carried him back to safety. Unfortunately, his friend had died on the way back to base camp. "I told you it wasn't worth the risk. He's dead," said the commander. "Oh, no," Jim said, "I'm glad I went. Just as I came to him he said, 'Jim, I knew you'd be back. I knew I could count on you.'"[6]

If we think about it, we realize we need to be faithful to those around us who need the Lord. "A truthful witness does not deceive, but a false witness pours out lies" (Prov. 14:5). "And the things you have heard me say in the presence of many witnesses entrust to reliable men who will also be qualified to teach others" (2 Tim. 2:2). We have been given the gospel as a great gift. It's meant to be shared. We should pass the gospel on to others. Are we a part of those faithful people who pass the gospel on to others?

Americans love a good story! Really, I think all humans love a story. The story of the *Titanic* has a lasting appeal and fascination to us. On April 15, 1912, 1,517 people were swallowed in the dark, icy waters of the ocean. The ship sank within the view of another ship. The officers of the *Californian* watched as the *Titanic* sank. They didn't have a clue about what was happening even though distress rockets had filled the sky for over an hour. The crew of the *Californian* were sleeping when the *Titanic* went down. The officers of the *Titanic* tried to establish radio contact with the *Californian*. The officer on duty called down the sleeping tube to his captain to notify him of the signals. The captain was asleep. Drowsily he asked, "Are they company signals?" The officer said, "I don't know." The captain went back to sleep. Just before 2:00 A.M. the *Titanic* desperately sent eight giant rockets arching in the sky. This time the young officer went to the captain's bed. "Were they white?" the captain asked. The young officer said, "All white." "What time is it?" the captain asked. "Two o' five," came the answer. He rolled over and went back to sleep. Perhaps many of the 1,517 who died could have been saved if people had been more faithful to their various duties. What about us? Churches and Christians today struggle for the souls of people. Are we faithful?

Do you know the Marine Corps motto? It is the well-known "Semper Fidelis"—meaning "Always Faithful." One year the theme for our youth ministry at First Baptist Church, Jacksonville, was "Found Faithful." May you and I always be found faithful as we share the good news of the gospel with others.

God blesses faithfulness. "A faithful man will be richly blessed, but one eager to get rich will not go unpunished" (Prov. 28:20). Many blessings come the way of the Christian who allows the Holy Spirit to produce the characteristic of faithfulness in his or her life. What about the blessing of helping others? The blessing of a personal sense of satisfaction that comes in doing one's duty to the best of one's ability? Or the blessing of winning the approval of the Lord?

I'm peeling faithfulness here. I'm finding it very appealing! Let's take another bite!

God Examines Faithfulness

One day God will examine our faithfulness. One of Jesus' most familiar parables teaches this. It is the parable of the talents (Matt. 25:14–30). Remember it? The talents discussed in the story do not refer to natural abilities. You may be able to sing beautifully or paint well. This is a talent, but it's not what Jesus is referring to in this story. As Jesus uses it, talents refer to opportunities for service. The three servants in the story are given different talents or opportunities. One was given five, the other was given two, and the last one was given only one talent. Obviously, this means not everyone has the same opportunities for service.

The story tells us that the three servants went to work at once, taking advantage of their opportunities. They were successful. The man with five gained five more. The man with two gained two more. Unfortunately, the man with just one took his opportunity and buried it in the earth.

Then we are told that the Lord of the servants returned and *reckoned with them* (Matt. 25:19). In other words, examination time had come. This teaches us that one day we will stand before God to show our use of the opportunities he has given to us. Look at the faithful servants in the parable. Their eyes are sparkling. They are pumped up with excitement. They are anxious for the Lord to see what they have done. The first one comes forward showing the Lord what he has done. He says, "I have gained five more" (v. 20). He is basically saying, "Look, Lord, here's what I have done with the opportunities you have given me." The man with the two opportunities says the same. The response of the Lord is marvelous. He says, "Well done good and faithful servant!" (v. 21). In other words, he is saying, "Excellent! Wonderful!" We learn here that praise from the Lord comes according to the faithfulness to the opportunities we have had. Surely these will be the sweetest words the Christian will ever hear: *Well done, faithful servant.*

Note also that the praise talks about a progression, moving from servant to ruler. If you are a faithful servant, then God will make you a ruler. This pattern is found consistently in the Bible. Moses spent forty years in the desert tending sheep. Did he ever look up to the Lord and say, "Excuse me, Lord. What's up? Have you forgotten me?" Moses was faithful as a servant, and the last forty years of his life were spent leading the nation of Israel.

How about Joseph? For about thirteen years Joseph was a slave and prisoner in Egypt. Was he bitter at the injustice and neglect he experienced?

No! He was faithful to his duties where he was. Before it was over, Joseph was prime minister of the land. Be faithful as a servant now, and God will enlarge your responsibilities later.

"Well done, good and faithful servant! You have been faithful with a few things; I will put you in charge of many things. Come and share your master's happiness!" (v. 21). What is your great joy? Faithfully serving Jesus? First comes the work, then comes the joy. OK, so maybe musical scales aren't the most fun aspect of practicing the piano. But hey, it's pretty cool to play Chopin or even Ray Charles music later on. There is little fun in hitting a blocking dummy on a steamy August afternoon. But it is way cool to score the winning touchdown on a fall Friday night!

As you probably know, the unfaithful servant didn't do so well. He buried his opportunity in the earth. Not the best plan. He had his eyes on the wrong world. Basically, he neglected the opportunity to do something to faithfully complete his duties. Too many Christians are so busy with the things of earth that they neglect opportunities to be faithful to the Lord.

I believe that God is going to examine our faithfulness in little things. Why? In Luke 16:10 Jesus talks about "very little" and "much." God is watching to see how we do with the little things he gives us. David, as a young man, took cheese to his brothers. He was faithful to do a little task. Later on David placed millions in the hands of Solomon to build a temple. He was faithful in the small things, and God gave him opportunities to be faithful on a bigger scale.

The first attempt to cut the Panama Canal through the mountains of Panama ended in failure. Yes, they began tackling the mountains, but they abandoned the project because of the mosquitoes. Yellow fever killed thousands of workers. American doctors then found a way to protect people from the mosquitoes. Once the little mosquitoes were taken care of, the mountains were conquered and the canal was soon finished. God will trust us with big things when he sees he can trust us in the little things.

"Master, where shall I work today?"

And my love flowed warm and free.

And he pointed to a little spot and said,
"Tend that for me."
"Not that little spot," I said. "None of my friends will see."
But he wept as he sent me back and said,
"Are you serving them or me?
Nazareth was a little place.
And so was Galilee."
— Author unknown

God is not going to ask if you were noticed. He is not going to ask how much work you did. But I do believe he is going to ask, "Were you faithful to what I called you to do, where I placed you to do it, and when I asked you to do it?" God examines faithfulness. This is important stuff. Faithfulness is where the rubber meets the road in the Christian life.

God will crown faithfulness. "Do not be afraid of what you are about to suffer. I tell you, the devil will put some of you in prison to test you, and you will suffer persecution for ten days. Be faithful, even to the point of death, and I will give you the crown of life" (Rev. 2:10). Notice that he says, "Be faithful, even to the point of death," not until death. What does that mean? Christians should determine they would rather die than be unfaithful to the Lord.

There are far too many Roman candle Christians. I see them all the time. They start out bright and shining. They make a spectacular scene. Then they begin to sputter, to fizzle out, and to fall from the sky. Don't be a Roman candle Christian. Be a Christian who stays with it all the way to the end.

Christians are not called to be successful. We are called to be faithful. But what is true success? It is being faithful to the opportunities and abilities God gives us. You can be faithful. We are commanded to be faithful (1 Cor. 4:2; Rev. 2:10). But as always, when we try to be faithful, we realize our inadequacy. Exactly! We go to the Holy Spirit. As we yield our life to his control, we trust the one who is faithful to us to help us be faithful to him.

Your name may never be in *Forbes* magazine. You probably won't be featured on *Life Styles of the Rich and Famous*. You may not get in *Who's Who*—you might even show up in *Who's Not!* But if you are faithful to the Lord, you are a success. Just think about it. Going to heaven one day and hearing Jesus say, "Well done, thou good and faithful servant!" Faithfulness. How a-peeling!

CHAPTER 10

PEAK MEEKNESS

Sometimes there's a television commercial (or a *spot* as media people call it) that just stands out. We remember the commercial because it's witty or because it starts some new catch phrase. It shows us just how powerful media images are in our lives. Some of these commercials are remembered and even quoted for years to come.

Do you remember the one for Polaner All-Fruit? This polite, mannerly lady is hosting a dinner party. All the folks at the table look really classy and civilized. So they start eating. Different guests say in their nicest voices, "Please pass the All-Fruit." All is fine until one country bumpkin at the table says, "Please pass the jelly." Of course, everyone at the table is shocked at his faux pas, but he definitely communicates his need.

I think I remember that commercial because it advertises something to die for—strawberry preserves. I love strawberries! They're *the bomb*, and they're good for you too. Did you know that the strawberry is the most popular of all berries? I believe it because I'm one who loves to eat strawberries!

The Latin name for strawberry, *fraga*, refers to the fruit's wonderful, enticing fragrance. Some say the English word *strawberry* comes from the straw used between the rows to keep the berries clean and to protect them in the wintertime. Others say it was originally *strewberry*, because the berries appear to be strewn or scattered among the leaves of the plant. What do you think?

The strawberry is unusual because its seeds are embedded in the surface rather than protected within the berry. That's why strawberries feel rough to the touch. The sweetest and most nutritious strawberries are those which have been sun-ripened on the plant, increasing the amount of vitamin C.

Strawberries are really good for us. They're important to cardiac health. They offer nutritional energy easy for the body to digest and process. Strawberries are also known as a skin-cleansing food. Some say that cut strawberries rubbed on the face after washing will remove sunburns. No, I haven't tried that one yet. Maybe you should try it and let me know how it works out.

Strawberries are easy to grow and easy to pick! No ladder is needed. They are planted, and they grow in the ground. In fact, you have to stoop down to get them.[1]

It seems to me like an act of meekness to bend down to pick up a straw-berry. It's almost as though the human picker is humbling himself or herself before the fruit of the earth. Because of this act of meekness, a peak crop can be enjoyed. Likewise, the peak Christian life comes about through meekness. I like to call it Peak Meekness.

What's meekness? I'm talking about the fruit of the Spirit meekness. Meekness requires that we stoop down. Meekness has a cleansing effect on the windows of our lives so that the beauty of Jesus may be seen in us.

Was meekness or gentleness popular in the New Testament world? Not exactly! Many have noted that it was the most unpopular and least desirable of all the Christian virtues. Why? I think it is because its meaning is not understood.

So what is meekness or gentleness? First, let's see what it isn't. Unfortunately, meekness rhymes with weakness. People get the idea they mean the same thing: to be meek is to be weak; to be weak is to be meek. But they don't. Meekness does not mean being spineless. Some look upon meekness as a lack of strength or courage. The milquetoast personality like that of a Peewee Herman is considered meek. But the gentle individual is not some insipid, wimpy character. In fact, uncommon strength is needed to be meek. Meekness is reasonable but never weak. It is willing to yield, but it is never spineless.

Meekness really is hard to define. Barclay says it is one of the most untranslatable words. The word actually conveys three main ideas. First, it means "to be submissive to the will of God." Second, it means "to have a teachable spirit." The meek person is one who is not too proud to learn. And third, and most often, meekness conveys the idea of "being considerate." That's some definition for this weak word! Aristotle said meekness was the quality of being angry at the right time and never angry at the wrong time.[2] Sanders conveys the same idea by saying that meekness is "anger on a leash."[3] Chew on that one! George defines gentleness as "a submissive and teachable spirit toward God that manifests itself in genuine humility and consideration towards others."[4] The best definition for meekness I have read is strength under control. Gentleness is power harnessed in loving service and respectful actions.

Does your mind ever picture certain objects or ideas when a certain word is mentioned? Well, several word pictures are indicated by gentleness. Think about wind. It's strong and powerful, yet sometimes it is a gentle breeze, cooling and refreshing. The ingredients of a certain medicine in and of themselves are powerful and may kill a human. Yet, when blended they produce a soothing cure. Gentleness would be the word to describe the soothing medicine. Or think about a tamed animal. The horse, for example, is strong and courageous. But broken, domesticated, and responsive to its master's control, it becomes gentle. Power under control. Maybe you consider your computer to be the same way. Megahertz under control! Maybe I should launch a new line of computers called "meek machines." What do you think?

OK, maybe not! Let's get back to the definition. Gentleness moves in two directions. It has a God-ward aspect. To be gentle is to be completely trusting and submissive to God. The gentle person is one willing to leave everything in the hands of God. Second, the word moves toward people. In that sense, it is a quality of mildness in dealing with others. Definitely needed in today's consumer culture!

The best Old Testament example of gentleness I know is Moses. "Now Moses was a very humble man, more humble than anyone else on the face of the earth" (Num. 12:3). Moses was far from a weak man. But he was mighty because he was meek. How do we know? We are told Moses was gentle when his brother and sister were giving him a hard time because of his wife. In the midst of this sticky situation Moses showed great strength and reserve. When his sister was stricken with leprosy, he implored God, "O God, please heal her!" (Num. 12:13).

The Lord Jesus is the best New Testament example of gentleness as stated in three references to gentleness related to Jesus. "Take my yoke upon you and learn from me, for I am gentle and humble in heart, and you will find rest for your souls" (Matt. 11:29). "See your king comes to you, gentle and riding on a donkey, on a colt, the foal of a donkey" (Matt. 21:5). "By the meekness and gentleness of Christ, I appeal to you . . ." (2 Cor. 10:1). Was Jesus weak? Follow him into the temple. See him turn over the tables of the money changers. Watch him drive out robbers with his whip. No weakness. Meekness is power under control.

The fruit of the Spirit is gentleness. This spiritual meekness is a trait only the Holy Spirit can produce in and through us as we yield to him.

The Origin of Meekness

Meekness is not exactly natural to the human heart. Human beings are really good at expressing pride and arrogance. But meekness? No way! Gentleness grows only when the human heart is a garden made by God and cultivated by the Holy Spirit.

Where does it come from? "For the Lord takes delight in his people; he crowns the humble with salvation" (Ps. 149:4). Gentleness is something which comes about through the salvation experience. Psalm 45:4 (KJV) uses *meekness* with two other words, *truth* and *righteousness*. The truth is, we are sinners and need a Savior. In meekness we surrender ourselves to that gospel truth. As a result, God makes us righteous!

When a person, in gentleness, receives Christ into his or her life; the Holy Spirit produces and develops gentleness. The Holy Spirit teaches us to accept discipline and authority. He helps us exercise meekness toward God and toward other people. Our spirit begins to accept God's dealings with us because we realize his will is good and best for us.

In all reality, the awareness of what God has done for us when he saved us should produce a spirit of meekness in us. I read about this French leader who rose from a humble background as a shepherd to a position of leadership in his nation. In his home he kept a room called his "Shepherd's room," where he kept reproductions of the hills and the valleys, the streams and the rocks, and the sheepfolds of his former life. There he kept the staff he had carried and the clothes he wore as a shepherd. One day, when asked the meaning of this Shepherd's room he replied, "If ever my heart is tempted to haughtiness and pride, I go into that room and remind myself of what I once was."[5]

Jesus said, "Blessed are the meek . . ." (Matt. 5:5). There seems to be special blessings from God given to those who are meek. What kind of blessings? Joy is one. "The meek also shall increase their joy in the Lord . . ." (Isa. 29:19 KJV). A person who meekly surrenders to the Lord has a depth of joy others do not experience. Maybe one of the daytime talk shows could talk about that. I can hear it now. "Today, guests who experience joy deeper than anybody else!" It would be neat, wouldn't it? Guidance is another blessing to the meek. "The meek will he guide in judgment: and the meek will he teach his way" (Ps. 25:9 KJV). When we submit to God, he is thrilled to guide and direct our lives. Provision is another blessing to the meek. "The meek shall eat and be satisfied: they shall praise the Lord that seek him . . ." (Ps. 22:26 KJV). As we submit daily to the Lord, he provides the needs of our lives. This is why Jesus taught us to daily come to God in prayer, asking for each day's needs.

The Obligation of Meekness

Timothy George says, "One who is gentle will not attempt to push others around or arrogantly impose one's own will on subordinates or peers. But gentleness is not incompatible with decisive action and firm convictions."[6] Gentleness is primarily a trait that enables us to respond properly to other people. We should show meekness in the ministry that God has given to us. "To slander no one, to be peaceable and considerate, and to show true humility toward all men" (Titus 3:2). "But you, man of God, flee from all this, and pursue righteousness, godliness, faith, love, endurance and gentleness" (1 Tim. 6:11). Gentleness is especially needed by those who serve the Lord in places of ministry. The gentle leader really has a special power. There is something disarming and refreshing about meekness. People respond to it positively. Gentleness defuses a bad temper. The quiet, meek answer has a way of calming a turbulent situation. Gentle leaders simply don't have to argue. There is an absence of retaliation in leaders who are meek. Briscoe says, "Meekness is the strength of backing off from a fight you could win and a point you could nail down, for the sake of the damage that would be done and the greater issues at stake."[7]

In an interesting passage, 1 Peter 3:1–4 talks about meekness in a marriage. The setting here is a wife seeking to win an unsaved husband to the Lord. The husband does not read the Bible. He's not interested. He doesn't go to church to hear the Word preached. What's a godly wife to do? Nag him? No. Browbeat him? No. Her beauty should be "the unfading beauty of a gentle and quiet spirit, which is of great worth in God's sight" (v. 4). This spirit can have a powerful impact on an unsaved mate.

Really, everything about our manner as Christians should indicate gentleness. "Be completely humble and gentle; be patient, bearing with one another in love" (Eph. 4:2). Our daily life should be about walking in gentleness. "Who is wise and understanding among you? Let him show it by his good life, by deeds done in the humility that comes from wisdom" (James 3:13). Our daily activities should show gentleness. Even our words of witness should be characterized by gentleness. "But in your hearts set apart Christ as Lord. Always be prepared to give an answer to everyone who asks you to give the reason for the hope that you have. But do this with gentleness and respect" (1 Pet. 3:15). In our witness to lost people, the grace of gentleness is vital. A genuine and meek Christian witness has a greater chance for a favorable reception than a rude, arrogant one. Yes, it is easy for Christians to get short or even proud with the lost: "We have the truth, and we know it. We have the answers to life and we want to share them." Because of this we may not show the considerate spirit we needed in our witnessing. But we are not here to win shouting matches. We are here to win souls to Jesus Christ.

So how do we get this gentleness? Jesus invites us to learn meekness from him. "Take my yoke upon you and learn from me, for I am gentle and humble in heart, and you will find rest for your souls" (Matt. 11:29). This verse represents a beautiful picture. To yoke up meant to become a disciple. The context refers to a younger ox being placed in a yoke with an older, more experienced ox. They walk and work together in step. So Jesus is saying, "Submit your life to me. Walk and work with me. Let me teach you how to be meek." What is his yoke like? He says it fits well. You may know that an ox yoke was made of wood. It was tailor-made for the animal. It fits perfectly so as not to wear or rub the neck. Jesus is saying that yoking up with him is not a tedious experience but a delightful one. Learning meekness from Jesus, one step at a time, brings us joy and great fulfillment in this life. "O may that mind in us be formed which shone so bright in Thee; a humble, meek and lowly mind, from pride and envy free" (author unknown).

The Bible gives us some examples of areas where we can show gentleness. Remember that gentleness is not so much what we do as how we do it. That's important. We are not talking about actions so much as attitudes. Our response to God's Word is an opportunity for meekness. "Therefore, get rid of all moral filth and the evil that is so prevalent and humbly accept the word planted in you, which can save you" (James 1:21). Christians should not treat the Word of God with indifference. We are to submit to it, to be changed by it. The Word of God does us no good if we do not receive it. And we do not receive it unless we have a teachable spirit. When your pastor preaches the Word on Sunday, are you teachable? As your Sunday school teacher presents the Bible study in your Sunday school class, are you willing to submit to its truth? In your daily devotions, as you read the Scriptures, do you receive with a gentle spirit what God shows you there? If you do, then you're on your way. The Word of God will bring great blessing and benefit to your life. How do you know if you have a teachable spirit? Verse 22 gives the answer: "Do not merely listen to the word, and so deceive yourselves. Do what it says." You're developing meekness when you begin to not only read the Word, but live the Word also in your daily life.

What else do we know about meekness? Well, it can be shown in the restoration of those who have wandered from the Lord. "Brothers, if someone is caught in a sin, you who are spiritual should restore him gently. But watch yourself, or you also may be tempted" (Gal. 6:1). Sometimes, Christians fall out of fellowship with the Lord. They wander away. Sin overcomes them. They make poor choices. Christians are to have a ministry of restoration to these wandering Christians. Yet to minister effectively, they must have an understanding spirit, not a condemning spirit.

Often Christians who wander away are seeking restoration. The word *restore* has an interesting background. It refers to a surgeon setting a broken bone. Ever had a broken bone? I have. I broke my big toe one time. Talk about painful. I went to the emergency room. A young intern saw that my big toe was obviously broken. He grabbed it and tried to yank it back in line. Yowza! I hit the roof! When you have a broken bone you don't exactly want a doctor who jerks and yanks it. You want him to be gentle. Tender. Easy. Well, in a way, we are spiritual surgeons. We should seek to help people come back into line. But we should do this gently. Why? "But watch yourself." Remember as you deal with wandering Christians, "that could be me." We are all capable of failing, and many of us will fail along the way. When we do, let's pray some Christian with a meek spirit will do the restoration work.

The Outcome of Meekness

Jesus said in Matthew 5:5, "Blessed are the meek." But he continued, "for they will inherit the earth." What does that mean? It means God esteems meekness. Remember 1 Peter 3 and the gentle spirit of the believing wife seeking to win her lost husband? The verse continues, "that meekness in the sight of God of great price." Why? When we are meek we are learning to think as God thinks. Gentleness sees as God sees. Gentleness feels as God feels.

What's all that about the meek inheriting the earth? Well actually, this world belongs to God's children. We see things others just don't see. Many people who do not know the Lord never really see or appreciate God's beautiful world. They go through the day and never have any understanding or appreciation for what God has provided for them. But knowing the Lord gives you a new set of eyes—eyes that are directed to the Holy Spirit. Common sights and sounds take on a new meaning. "The poor will eat and be satisfied; they who seek the Lord will praise him—may your hearts live forever!" (Ps. 22:26). The meek inherit the earth now, but there is also a future aspect.

"The LORD sustains the humble but casts the wicked to the ground" (Ps. 147:6). Many times Christians are often treated with contempt and viewed as worthless or not seen at all. That's OK. Such an evaluation is for a time only. People who do not know the Lord have no clue of what the believer really possesses. Their take is all about what gentleness misses, and they may fail to see what gentleness produces. Jesus says that the future is bright for the meek. They will inherit the earth.

Even nature teaches us that the meek inherit the earth. Ever visited a museum? Did you see those huge dinosaur remains? Those were some big boys! There was a time when those huge dinosaurs seemed to rule the earth. They ruled simply to devour and kill. Yet if you look around, you see lowly sheep, passive cows, and working horses. They are humble, but they render valuable services. The dinosaurs are gone. The lowly ones have inherited the earth. How about that?

History also teaches us that the meek inherit the earth. What happens to world leaders? Where do they end up? Herod, Napoleon, and Alexander, where are they now? They seemed to inherit the earth in their day. But did they? They are gone now. But there is one who said, *I am meek and lowly in heart*. And he is alive forever more. He is worshiped the world over. He is King of kings and Lord of lords. The meek and lowly One has inherited the earth. The good news is that you are going to inherit the earth with him.

The Bible commands us to wear meekness or put it on like a garment. "Therefore, as God's chosen people, holy and dearly loved, clothe yourselves with compassion, kindness, humility, gentleness and patience" (Col. 3:12). It also commands us to pursue meekness. "But you, man of God, flee from all this, and pursue righteousness, godliness, faith, love, endurance and gentleness" (1 Tim. 6:11). So this drives us once again to the Holy Spirit. We cannot successfully obey the command to gentleness on our own. We need help. The Holy Spirit must produce this fruit in and through our lives.

Have you ever read the Old Testament story of Abraham and Lot? God blessed both of them. So much so that they had to separate and go different ways. Abraham was the uncle. Lot was the nephew. Abraham could have pulled rank and made the first choice. But he didn't. Abraham was meek. He allowed Lot the first choice. So Lot lifted up his eyes and chose all that his eyes could see. Unfortunately he, as many of us have done, made a bad choice. His selfishness led him to Sodom. Abraham left the choice to God. The result? God told him he would give him everything his eyes could see. Actually, Abraham left the choice up to God. So he was given all God's eyes could see! The meek indeed shall inherit the earth.

Baskets of meekness. You have to stoop down to get them. But once you do they have a cleansing effect on your life. As the Spirit produces his gentleness in and through us, other people are better able to see the One who said, *I am meek and lowly in heart*.

Be meek and be at your peak!

CHAPTER 11

APROPOS APRICOT

Yes, I do like the grocery store. Laugh at me. I don't care. I can't help it. I particularly love the shapes and sizes, colors and packaging you see in the produce section. Some people go to airports for fun. I go to grocery stores.

One of my favorite fruits is the sun-dried apricots. I think they are packaged very attractively in an apropos manner. In other words, I think the packaging is appropriate for the fruit inside. In this case, we're talking about apricots.

Did you know that apricots are native to China? They were introduced to the Greco-Roman world by Alexander the Great around the fourth century B.C. In the early 1700s Franciscan friars brought apricots to California, and even today most of our apricots come from that state.

Apricots cook beautifully. You can use them in sauces, jellies, jams, and chutneys. Yes, I like chutney too! Apricots are delicious baked with pies, tarts, and cakes. I enjoy them added to my ice cream, my fruit salad, and my cereal. They have a sweet taste with a tart edge. They're edgy. But they're apropos too. Apricots really are not all that noticeable at first glance, yet they pack a punch. Perhaps apricots are "flavor under control." Or you might say apricots practice self-control.

Apricots provide many health benefits. They are a good source for vitamins A and C. They contain highly concentrated amounts of beta-carotene, which some believe helps prevent lung and skin cancers. Because they build red corpuscles in the blood, they also fight disorders such as anemia and acne.[1]

Do you think Alexander the Great ate apricots? I bet he did. He really was a great leader. He ruled Macedonia at age 16, and at 18 he was a victorious general. He became a king at the young age of 20. He mastered the world's continents, yet he was never able to truly master or control himself. He was a slave to his passions and died young. Perhaps he could have learned a lesson from the apropos apricot.

The fruit of the Spirit is self-control, and it is the last of the nine graces of character Paul lists for us in Galatians 5:22–23. Remember the first one, *love?* It fulfills the Hebrew ideal. This last one *self-control* fulfills the Greek ideal. See, self-control was lacking in the New Testament world when Paul was writing his letters. It was a wild time. Sexual excess, gluttony in eating, and anger and violence in behavior and words were prevalent. Paul was in a culture totally out of control. So Paul taught new believers about self-control. Doesn't this remind you of today? Yes, our society is out of control. Many people are like missiles off course. What about road rage? It is a major problem today. People can't control their anger behind the wheel. What about the excessive drinking and sexual extremes we see wrecking lives today? Thousands of people have trouble controlling money. Personal consumer debt is at an all-time high. That little plastic one-ounce credit card can actually control a big man or a grown woman. We live in an undisciplined, out-of-control age. People seek freedom through excess, but they find only bondage. They seek pleasure through releasing their passions, but find pain instead.

The King James Bible says the fruit of the Spirit is *temperance*. Really that means "self-control." The Greek word literally means "holding in with a firm hand, taking hold of or having under control." It is found only six times in the New Testament. As an adjective, it is found in Titus 1:8, Galatians 5:23, Acts 24:25, and 2 Peter 1:6. As a verb, it is found in 1 Corinthians 7:9 and 9:25.

What is self-control all about? Barclay translates it "self-mastery." He defines it as "the virtue which makes a man so master himself that he is fit to be the servant of others."[2] Timothy George says that self-control refers to "the mastery of our desires and passions."[3] Peterson defines it as "the freedom to discipline and direct our energies wisely."[4] Briscoe's definition of self-control is more elaborate. He says it means to "handle all that would mar our lives before God. . . . It involves handling freedom properly. . . . It means I say no to all that God forbids and yes to all that He ordains."[5]

Perhaps a good, concise definition of self-control is "the mastery of our total self." Did you ever get in trouble for talking too much in school? I did in second grade! The teacher told my parents, "Jerry needs to practice self-control." The idea here is letting one's appetites, passions, and impulses be under the control of the Holy Spirit. Sanders says that it is "the quality which perhaps more than others, differentiates man from the lower animals."[6] How about the apricots?

Self-control covers all of our emotions and passions. It suggests control of body, spirit, and soul. With self-control, we can hold back from all that is wrong. We can also weigh what is best and make the best choice. The idea is moderation in all the things that are good for us and abstinence from all the things that are bad for us. It's all about having our desires under control. That's self-control.

Self-control is another one of the characteristics we should add to our Christian life. Second Peter 1:5–6 says, "For this very reason, make every effort to add to your faith goodness; and to goodness, knowledge; and to knowledge, self-control; and to self-control, perseverance; and to perseverance, godliness."

How Self-control Is Contrasted

Self-control is contrasted to *the works of the flesh* mentioned previously in Galatians 5. What's that got to do with this SpiritFruit? Well, the different works of the flesh show a serious lack of self-control. A car out of control means death on the highway, right? A fire out of control means beautiful trees in the forest are destroyed. But a person out of control is even worse. He or she wrecks lives and breaks relationships. What are some of these works of the flesh? Sexual immorality—sex out of control. Idolatry—worship out of control. Wrath—anger out of control. Drunkenness—appetite out of control.

Paul understood that self-control is necessary to the successful Christian life. So he includes it as a part of a genuine presentation of the gospel. Christ changes our past and our future. But the clincher is that we are to allow him to change our present. How? Yield to the Holy Spirit, who wants to produce the fruit of self-control in our lives.

The Bible gives us several examples of people whose lives were out of control. Samson. Remember him? Now there's a *man!* One of the strongest men who ever lived, but what a tragic life! He could conquer thousands of men, but he could not conquer the passions of his own life. His lack of self-control robbed him of personal strength and the power of the Holy Spirit in his life. He made some very bad choices. I often think that Samson had the greatest potential of any person in the Old Testament. What could he have been if he had learned self-control? No man could conquer him—including himself! Samson won victories over his enemies on the outside. He couldn't win victories over himself on the inside. His life was uncontrolled lust and fits of anger, driven by carnal desire. He let his passions control him, and he brought shame to his family and personal disgrace to himself. As we read his sad story we find ourselves wanting to shout, "Yo, Samson! Smell the coffee. What is up with you, Samson? Are you insane?"

The New Testament tells us about Felix. He is an example of a person who lacked self-control. Felix and Druscilla heard one of Paul's sermons. Acts 24:25 tells us the outline of his message. He preached to them about a righteousness that they did not possess and about a judgment to come for which they were not prepared. But he also preached to them about—you guessed it—self-control. They weren't exactly big fans of self-control. Felix's name means happy. Yet Felix was anything but happy. He had endured three miserable marriages. He stayed in debt constantly. His life was a round of wild parties. Sound like people today? Druscilla had married a king when she was fourteen. Felix became enamored with her. A sorcerer helped him seduce her from her husband. I can imagine that Paul told her she had lost everything important in a woman's life: decency, modesty, purity. I also bet Paul told Felix that though Felix could not control his passions on his own, Jesus Christ could control them.

There is quite a contrast between a life controlled by Christ and a life out of control. Proverbs 25:28 says, "Like a city whose walls are broken down / is a man who lacks self-control." What is the purpose of walls? Why do we build them? For protection. But when our lives are out of control, we are just like a city without walls, open to the enemies of our souls: the world, the flesh, and the devil.

Do you like tests? I do! Did you ever take a personality test? The Taylor-Johnson Temperament Analysis reveals interesting aspects of personality. It shows what traits a person has or lacks. For example, it can show that a person who lacks self-control has other problems as well. A lack of self-control causes one to suffer from nervousness, depression, self-centeredness, and a critical disposition. For example, think about people who buy on impulse. They cannot control the urge to buy. They see something they want, the urge hits them hard, and—boom—they spend money—usually plastic! They pull out a credit card and shout like a soldier, "Charge!" They are out of control! Then nervousness and reality set in. "What if I can't make the payments?" Then they become really depressed that they let it happen to them again. They realize how selfish and self-centered they are, and they become very critical of themselves. Lack of self-control brings with it a multitude of other problems.

So Paul shows self-control to be a needed trait of the Spirit-controlled character. Yes, there is a major contrast between being in and out of control!

How Self-control Is Presented

In the New Testament self-control is presented as a very powerful characteristic—one that reminds us of our humanity. Lack of self-control is actually a part of our old nature. If a Christian lacks self-control, it is a sign that the old nature is dominating. It is a sign of carnality, letting the old nature run the show.

You know, our culture is out of control. People often do whatever they want. Jesus said, "Deny yourself." Our culture says, "Indulge yourself." We all need self-control in so many ways. We need it physically, don't we? What about food? Consume in moderation, not in dissipation. Be disciplined and get proper exercise. I know it may mean getting up and out there early, but it's worth it! Self-control is important emotionally as well. Learning to keep emotional passion and moral control is very important. This is all about using self-control to follow the moral guidelines given to us in God's Word.

Proverbs 16:32 says, "Better a patient man than a warrior, a man who controls his temper than one who takes a city." Peter the Great, in a fit of anger one day, hit his gardener so hard he died. Afterward he was filled with remorse. He said, "Alas, I have civilized my own subjects, I have conquered other nations, yet I have not been able to civilize nor conquer myself."[7]

Self-control is not presented in the Bible as a result of our efforts. Rather, self-control is the fruit of the Spirit. There's no way to gain control over self by one's self. The Stoics taught a type of self-mastery. It was about a morbid suppression of the desires. They came to the point of worshiping their own self-will. That's not SpiritFruit self-control. Christian legalism does the same thing. In Colossians 2 Paul mentions those who worship their own self-will. He points out in Colossians 2:23 how futile it is to try to live the Christian life by one's own power of will. This is why Christian legalism really doesn't work. It emphasizes what we do or what we fail to do instead of the power of the Holy Spirit, who can control our passions and desires.

Self-control is really about bringing our whole life under the Holy Spirit's control. It is not the outward result of self-repression but rather the inward result of the Spirit's work. The Bible puts it this way, "So I say, live by the Spirit, and you will not gratify the desires of the sinful nature. For the sinful nature desires what is contrary to the Spirit, and the Spirit what is contrary to the sinful nature. They are in conflict with each other, so that you do not do what you want" (Gal. 5:16–17). As we allow the Holy Spirit to live the Christian life in and through us, then he gives us power to control the desires and passions of our human nature.

The Holy Spirit can help us control our speech. The tongue has power to produce life and the power to produce death. James 3:6 pictures the tongue as a fire that can burn and do great damage when it is out of control. Second Corinthians 10:5 talks about bringing even our thoughts, which precede our words, into captivity by Christ. Now we're talking about self-control, and the Holy Spirit can help us control our thought life and our speech. Someone said that the soul is dyed by the color of our thoughts. That statement really is true, isn't it?

The Holy Spirit can also help us control sexual desire. In Scripture, self-control is closely related to sexual impulses and desires. In fact, 1 Corinthians 7:9 deals with this topic: "But if they cannot control themselves, they should marry, for it is better to marry than to burn with passion."

All of life has the potential for great evil or for great good. When our desires, emotions, and feelings are out of control, great evil can come about. Under control, these emotions and feelings can produce great good. A fire out of control can burn down a house. But fire under control can cook a meal or warm a house on a snowy evening. Sexual desire out of control can result in great evil. Relationships can be wrecked. Bodies can be racked with disease. Under control, sexual desire can make a marriage fulfilling and bring into the world beautiful children.

The advantages of practicing self-control far outweigh the disadvantages. For the person who has no control over his or her desire for alcohol, the hangover and other attendant problems may be worth it for a time. But in the long run, these problems aren't worth it. For the person who cannot control the desire for illicit sexual encounters, the guilt, the disease, and the sorrow created are a very high price to pay.

Did your mom have certain wise sayings you still remember? Whenever you had a little fight with any friends or thought that things just weren't going your way, my mom would say, "You've got to learn to act, not react!" It took me a long time to understand the profound truth of that statement. Likewise, when we're faced with decisions now, we should ask ourselves several questions when our desires want us to move in certain directions. "Is this helpful?" "Is this constructive?" "Will this glorify God?"

I think about how controlled Jesus lived in his earthly life. He was God in human flesh, and so many opportunities came his way to demonstrate a lack of self-control. When he was mistreated, he could have lashed back. At his shameful trial, he could have exerted his power in extravagant, unbelievable ways. But he didn't. His was desire, passion, and power under control.

How Self-control Is Illustrated

The meaning and importance of self-control are illustrated in 1 Corinthians 9:25–27: "Everyone who competes in the games goes into strict training. They do it to get a crown that will not last; but we do it to get a crown that will last forever. Therefore I do not run like a man running aimlessly; I do not fight like a man beating the air. No, I beat my body and make it my slave so that after I have preached to others, I myself will not be disqualified for the prize." I like that because the illustration is taken from the world of sports. I am convinced that Paul was a sports fan! Go Jaguars! (Yes, I'm a fan, of course.) Evidently he regularly attended athletic events. He certainly used a lot of pictures from the world of competition. This one beautifully portrays the importance of self-control in our lives.

There are three stages to successful athletic activity. Stage one is training. This is the time when the athlete prepares for the competition. Training requires great self-control. The athlete must control his or her eating, sleeping, exercising, and practicing. I have such respect for Olympic athletes. They really do shame us. Mark Spitz won five gold medals for swimming. Once he was asked how much he trained. His response was that he swam the distance of several times around the world during his preparation.[8] That's swimming! Discipline is adherence to training with a sense of purpose. The athlete is willing to exercise this type of self-control because he or she has a goal in mind. The winner learns discipline because he or she wants to be the best.

Another aspect of successful athletic activity is competing. The time comes for the game itself. World-class athletes know how to compete under pressure with their skills under control. Without self-control a runner wanders aimlessly from side to side. Without control the boxer hits the air, but not the opponent. This reminds me of those who try to live the Christian life without self-control. They're all over the place!

The third aspect is winning. The athlete's goal in Paul's day was a fading laurel wreath. Times have changed, haven't they? There were also some perks. The winning athlete was allowed, along with his family, to be tax-free (that should encourage some self-control today!). He also became an applauded celebrity. Our incentives for living the Christian life successfully are different but have eternal results. Our crown doesn't fade. We compete because we have eternity in mind and seek to hear the Lord say, "Well done!"

God can give you control of your appetites and passions. The Bible teaches we are more than conquerors, and the Lord wants us to be conquerors, not the conquered. I remember hearing the sad comments of a young woman who was having a hard time. She said, "I have so many sins I don't know where to begin. I argue, and I complain. I spend money I don't have. I give in to the pressures to drink and to be sexually loose. I am a slave. I am dragging my chains around with me." It doesn't have to be this way.

God can give you the power to control the use of tobacco, alcohol, or drugs. He can help you control the passion to overeat. He can give you power to control your anger or sexual immorality. Interested? Want to know how to get there? It is not about imposing some set of rules on your life. Self-control does not develop by imposing outside rules. It comes by the indwelling of a Ruler on the inside. Galatians 5:24–25 says, "Those who belong to Christ Jesus have crucified the sinful nature with its passions and desires. Since we live by the Spirit, let us keep in step with the Spirit." Galatians 2:20 puts it this way. "I have been crucified with Christ and I no longer live, but Christ lives in me. The life I live in the body, I live by faith in the Son of God, who loved me and gave himself for me."

In Homer's epic, *The Odyssey*, Ulysses returns from battle and, on the way, passes an island inhabited by the Sirens. These beautiful, seductive young women sang so alluringly they attracted men to their island and to destruction. Ulysses tried to prevent the disaster by plugging the ears of his soldiers with wax. Jason, another character, had a better way. He had Orpheus play music on his harp, music even sweeter than the Siren song. It overrode the song of the Sirens, and he and his crew passed safely.

That applies to the Christian life too. We do not conquer our passions by rules on the outside; we conquer by death to self on the inside.

A little child was memorizing the list of fruits of the Spirit. As she quoted them she came to the last one and said, "Remote-control." Not too far from right! That kid is up to date. If Jesus has remote-control, we can have self-control.

I often think about Jesus in the garden of Gethsemane. He presented a beautiful picture of self-control. You can see the Son of God bringing his whole physical, emotional, and spiritual being into total subjection to the will of God. At the climax of it all, he says, *Not my will, but thine be done*. That's self-control. How did Jesus do that? How could he surrender himself to the cross the night before and go to a sure death the next day? Hebrews 9:14 says, "How much more, then, will the blood of Christ, who through the eternal Spirit offered himself unblemished to God, cleanse our consciences from acts that lead to death, so that we may serve the living God!" That's the kind of control the Holy Spirit wants to produce in and through our lives. And that's where power comes from!

Frederick the Great of Prussia was walking one afternoon around the outskirts of Berlin. He met an old man walking toward him. "Old man, who are you?" asked Frederick. The old man replied, "Why, I am a king." Frederick laughed, "A king! Over what kingdom do you reign?" The old man proudly replied, "Over myself."

Remember that 2 Peter 1:5–6 commanded us to add self-control to our Christian life? How do we do that? We go to the Holy Spirit. He alone can give us self-control.

Have a package of self-control. It is sweet to the taste, and it will put strength in your soul. Live the good life. Live a self-controlled life.

You know, I'm getting hungry. I think I'll head over to the produce section in the supermarket.

CHAPTER 12

FRUIT IN FULL

The famous author Tom Wolfe recently wrote a novel entitled *Man in Full*. In it, he tells of a man named Charlie Croker who really had it all. The aging Georgia Tech football star enjoyed the praise of adoring fans all around him. He went on to build a real estate empire. The crown jewel of his empire was a massive building in northern Atlanta modestly called Croker Tower.

You can probably guess the rest of the story. He had a much younger "trophy" wife who stole him from the mother of his children. This new wife dragged Charlie with her from social event to fund raiser to charity ball. To many, Charlie did have it all—even his own jet and a plantation for hunting in south Georgia. Charlie was a man in full.

Sometimes this sort of American Dream doesn't last, and Charlie's didn't. His real estate empire collapsed. His businesses lost millions. He struggled to keep from going bankrupt. But he crashed and burned.

Know what happened next? Surprise. He became an evangelist! For Jesus, you ask? Nope! He became an evangelist for an ancient, mythological god named Zeus! Good grief, Charlie Croker? What was up with this man in full? You know, maybe Tom Wolfe should have named his book *A Man in Folly!*

As I think more about Wolfe's book title, I realize Jesus is truly a "man in full." Jesus is God. He was God before he was born. He was God during his life on earth. He is God now, and he will always be God. He is fully God. But he is also man. The New Testament message is that when Jesus was born, God became flesh. John puts it like this, "The Word became flesh and made his dwelling among us. We have seen his glory, the glory of the One and Only, who came from the Father, full of grace and truth" (John 1:14). Jesus was fully God, but he was also fully man. What a concept! How do we deal with it? We deal with it by referring to Jesus as the God-man. He was everything a person should be. At the climax of his life, in the most divine and human expression of who Jesus is, the words were spoken, "Here is the man!" (John 19:5). See, the God-man on the cross showed Jesus in all his divine and human fullness.

Look at the life Jesus lived and you really do see fruit in full. We have been studying closely the fruit of the Spirit that Paul gave us in Galatians 5:22–23. When I look at this cluster of fruit in the Spirit, I always think of the Lord Jesus. Each aspect of the fruit of the Spirit points to him.

These nine graces teach us how our character can be shaped by the Holy Spirit's work of sanctification in us. As we have seen, the use of the singular word *fruit* for the cluster points to a unity and harmony of character produced in us by the Holy Spirit. The nine graces represent the successful Christian life fully controlled by the Holy Spirit. But they also point to the person of Christ and to the purpose of the Holy Spirit that is to make us like Jesus.

This ninefold picture of the fruit of the Spirit is a perfect display of Jesus. Did any other human being manifest this fruit in full? No. Only Jesus. Stuart Briscoe says, "The fruit of the Spirit is not a collection of unrelated fruits selected or neglected according to personal preference, but rather is a composite description of the all-around behavior which is the direct result of a unique relationship with the Living Lord who indwells His people by His Spirit."[1]

Think about a telescope. Its purpose is not to point to itself. Rather, its purpose is to bring the glorious heavens closer to us. Like the telescope, the purpose of the fruit of the Spirit is to show others the glories of the Lord Jesus Christ as his life is lived through us.

The graces of the Spirit picture the ideal Christian life. This ideal Christian is yielded to the Spirit's control so that people can see the virtues of Jesus. Once we are Christians, we should let the Holy Spirit work inside us and through us to produce all nine graces or manifestations of this fruit. That means Christ is reproduced in us! Cool! Paul puts it this way in Galatians 4:19, "My dear children, for whom I am again in the pains of childbirth until Christ is formed in you."

In this Man in full, Jesus, we see fruit in full. So let's summarize the nine graces of the Spirit as seen in the life of Jesus. Though the grouping is somewhat arbitrary, let's view the nine graces in three triads. The first three show us the Lord Jesus in his inward life. The middle three show us his outward life. The final three show us his upward life.

Jesus' Inward Life

Jesus is the only person who ever had a perfectly adjusted personality. Nothing about him was ruined by original sin. Jesus was virgin-born. Because of the virgin birth, the Holy Spirit short-circuited the sin cycle, and Jesus was born without sin. In addition, his personality was not damaged by sinful choices. ". . . but we have one who has been tempted in every way, just as we are—yet was without sin" (Heb. 4:15). So Jesus was filled with love, joy, and peace. How do we know? Consider the night before he was crucified. We see these three graces displayed in his inner life. Death is real. It brings reality to the human personality with a jolt! If there had been any cracks or faults in the Lord's personality, we would have seen them when he faced death.

Love

What about love? The night before the cross, can you see love in the life of the Lord Jesus? You bet! Even as he moves toward certain death, he speaks of love for his Father. Listen to him. "I in them and you in me. May they be brought to complete unity to let the world know that you sent me and have loved them even as you have loved me. 'Father, I want those you have given me to be with me where I am, and to see my glory, the glory you have given me because you loved me before the creation of the world'" (John 17:23–24). "I have made you known to them, and will continue to make you known in order that the love you have for me may be in them and that I myself may be in them" (v. 26). His love for the Father was displayed in full.

His heart was also filled with love for his disciples. John states this love in a unique way. In John 13:1 he says, ". . . Having loved his own who were in the world, he now showed them the full extent of his love." Literally, this could mean, "He loved them all the way." Jesus never stopped loving his disciples. Yet they were incredibly unlovely at times. You know they disappointed him. One of them even sold him for a few paltry pieces of silver. Did Jesus stop loving them? No way! He loved them all the way to Calvary!

God is the fountainhead of love, and Jesus is the perfect manifestation of love. How do we know? Well, think about love. How do we define it? One way to define love is to choose to do the best for another person. Listen to Jesus in John 15:13: "Greater love has no one than this, that he lay down his life for his friends." Jesus displays incredible love for us. Romans 5:8 says, "But God demonstrates his own love for us in this: While we were still sinners, Christ died for us." The word *commends* could be translated "displays, exhibits, or proves." Jesus proved his love for his disciples, for us, and for the world when he died on the cross.

In just a few hours he would be carried outside the city of Jerusalem. Cruel, calloused soldiers' hands would nail him to a cross. "For God so loved the world that he gave his one and only Son . . ." (John 3:16). I remember when I was a boy I played a little game with my friends called "I measure my love to you." Picture one of us standing in front of a person holding out our arms to a certain length. The length our arms were outstretched; this measured our love to the person. One day this boy was playing who had a crush on this little girl. He walked in front of her, stretched out his arms as wide as he could, and at the top of his voice shouted, "I measure my love to you." She just giggled, the way girls do. When Jesus stretched his arms out on the cross, reaching to the whole world, he wasn't playing this childish game. He was saying, "I love you this much."

You want to make it personal? OK. Jesus loves the world (John 3:16). Jesus loves the church (Eph. 5:25). But Paul makes it personal for us when he says, ". . . who loved me and gave himself for me" (Gal. 2:20). Yes, Jesus loves you, too!

When I was a kid, we occasionally sang the old hymn "Jesus Loves Even Me" in church: "I am so glad that our Father in heaven, / tells of his love in the Book he has given. / Wonderful things in the Bible I see. / This is the dearest that Jesus loves me." I can remember as if it were last night, singing the refrain at the top of my voice, "I am so glad that Jesus loves me, / Jesus loves me, Jesus loves me. / I am so glad that Jesus loves me. / Jesus loves even me." That just overwhelms me. It always has. It's about love in full from Jesus.

Joy

So what about joy? How could anyone be filled with joy the night before an expected brutal death? Well, read about it. "I have told you this so that my joy may be in you and that your joy may be complete" (John 15:11). "I tell you the truth, you will weep and mourn while the world rejoices. You will grieve, but your grief will turn to joy. A woman giving birth to a child has pain because her time has come; but when her baby is born she forgets the anguish because of her joy that a child is born into the world. So with you: Now is your time of grief, but I will see you again and you will rejoice, and no one will take away your joy. In that day you will no longer ask me anything. I tell you the truth, my Father will give you whatever you ask in my name. Until now you have not asked for anything in my name. Ask and you will receive, and your joy will be complete" (John 16:20–24). "I am coming to you now, but I say these things while I am still in the world, so that they may have the full measure of my joy within them" (John 17:13). The night before the cross, Jesus talked about joy. In fact, he said more about joy that night than at any other time.

Jesus displayed joy throughout his life. Though he was a "Man of sorrows," he was also a man of joy. Do you think Jesus had a sense of humor? I do! Our English versions do not always reflect the subtleties and nuances of the language Jesus used. The satire and irony in the words he used show that he was funny. Even with all the difficulties and disappointments Jesus encountered, he lived a life of full joy.

Everyone Jesus met and everywhere Jesus went, he left a load of joy behind. One of the great accusations brought against Jesus was that he associated with sinners. I assure you sinners didn't want a killjoy around.

Picture this! Jesus has reached the end of his earthly life. Nothing remains but a bare, brutal cross. From the lips of Jesus we hear only joy. And he can give you joy in full. ". . . your joy will be complete" (John 16:24). Also he can be "filled with an inexpressible and glorious joy" (1 Pet. 1:8).

Peace

Did Jesus have peace the night before the cross? You know it! "Peace I leave with you; my peace I give you. I do not give to you as the world gives. . . ." (John 14:27). "I have told you these things, so that in me you may have peace. In this world you will have trouble. But take heart! I have overcome the world" (John 16:33). The night before his death, he talked about peace, and he talked about peace after the cross. After he was raised from the dead, he spoke of his joy. We see references to joy three times in John 20.

Just what does peace mean? Peace means "total well-being." It means "to make complete or to bind together." Jesus had it all together. He was the complete man. You know, to be a true man, a man in full, there must be an inner tranquillity. You don't see that too often today! Yet we see full-throttled joy in Jesus the night before his death. His peace, or his sense of well-being and harmony, came because he was living in conformity to the will of God.

What about you? Well, Jesus can fill your life with peace also. Read John 14:27 again. "Peace I leave with you; my peace I give you. I do not give to you as the world gives. Do not let your hearts be troubled and do not be afraid." Even in your darkest hour, Jesus can fill you with his peace.

Jesus' Outward Life

Patience

When you think about patience, kindness, and goodness, who do you think about? You probably don't think about very many people. Yet these three expressions of the fruit are seen in our Lord's relationships with other people. In other words, Jesus' outward life showed these graces of the Spirit.

Take patience for instance. What does it really mean? It means "to be of long spirit." Jesus was long-suffering in his relationship with his disciples. Yes, they were some odd fellows! No two were alike. They were probably quite difficult to be around too! Selfish, petty, and boastful. They were slow to learn his teachings. They remind me of myself. Yet Jesus showed patience as he led and instructed them. It's not really natural for humans to be that way, you know!

Remember Simon the Zealot and Matthew the tax collector? They were disciples. They were also natural enemies. Jesus probably had to stop more than one argument between them. Remember Philip? He said to Jesus, "Lord, show us the Father and that will be enough for us" (John 14:8). Jesus patiently replied, "Philip, even after I have been among you such a long time?" (John 14:9).

What about James and John? Those guys were the Sons of Thunder.

Brothers. Both difficult to deal with in their own way. They actually had the gall to send their mother to Jesus to request the best seats in the kingdom (Matt. 20:20–28). That's confidence! Yet Jesus was so kind and patient with them.

And, of course, there's Peter. What a peacock! NBC would have hired him on the spot! So impetuous. Loud-mouthed. He had hoof-and-mouth disease. Every time he opened his mouth it was to change feet. Yet Jesus dealt patiently with him.

Then there was Judas, the thief. You know, he was actually stealing from the disciples' slush fund. He betrayed Jesus to the Jewish officials. Once again, Jesus showed patience. The night before the cross Jesus gave Judas the seat of honor. He extended to him the bread of friendship. The patience of Jesus is amazing.

Want something even more amazing? Jesus is patient with us today. He is so patient with me. If he had not been, I would be in hell right now.

Kindness

Patience is vital to the successful Christian life, but so is kindness. Kindness is "goodness of heart." It is a kindly disposition toward others that expresses itself through actions and words. Jesus showed kindness in many ways. The man at the pool of Bethesda had been sick for a really long time. No one had been kind enough to lift him in the water at the miracle time. Jesus didn't put him in the water. Not kind, you say? Well, Jesus put the water in him! That's kindness!

What about the woman at the well? Talk about a headache. There Jesus sat at Jacob's well, tired and thirsty. He asked her for a drink of water. She had one more smart mouth. Her hot, hateful words would have gotten her pushed in the well if I had been sitting there. But Jesus spoke kindly to her, and he is so kind to us.

Goodness

We definitely see kindness in the Lord's dealings with other people, but we also see goodness. Goodness is really "uprightness of heart and life." It is doing good in practical ways for others. We are told that Jesus "went around doing good" (Acts 10:38). When Jesus was near, people knew where to go for help.

I heard about a certain English nobleman named Sir Bartlee. He was known for his goodness. A stranger came to the city and looked for Sir Bartlee. Asking a passerby how to find and identify Sir Bartlee, he was told, "Look for the tall gentleman helping somebody."[2] Wouldn't you like for people to say that about you?

We really see Jesus' goodness in his relationships with sinners. Jesus was good to saved sinners like Simon Peter. For example, one day Jesus filled Peter's net with fish. Peter fell at the feet of Jesus exclaiming, *Depart from me, I'm a sinful man, O Lord.* Yet Jesus was good enough to put him on his evangelistic team. But Jesus was also good to lost sinners. The rich young ruler came to Jesus. He was interested in goodness. Jesus showed goodness to him by showing him the way to true goodness.

Aren't you glad God is good to us? Sometimes we sing a little chorus around our church, "God is so good. / God is so good. / God is so good. / He's so good to me." And he is.

Jesus' Upward Life

The last three graces are faithfulness, gentleness, and self-control. Jesus demonstrated these in full. How? Through his relationship with the heavenly Father.

Faithfulness

A faithful person is one you can rely on. Faithfulness carries the idea of "being reliable." A faithful person really means it when he or she says, "The check is in the mail." Faithfulness means "being dependable, or doing one's duty."

Jesus is referred to in Revelation as *the faithful witness* (Rev. 1:5). Jesus was completely faithful to God's task for him. At a young age Jesus said, "Didn't you know I had to be in my Father's house?" (Luke 2:49). He was always working while he was on earth to complete what the heavenly Father had given him to do. Before the cross he said, "I have brought you glory on earth by completing the work you gave me to do" (John 17:4). Then on the cross he exclaimed in victory, "It is finished" (John 19:30). Jesus really was totally and completely faithful to the heavenly Father. He showed faithfulness in full.

We should be faithful to the heavenly Father as well. Jesus gave us the model. He showed us how to do it. So all we have to do is allow the Holy Spirit to reproduce the life of Jesus in us, and he will help us to be faithful to God's purpose and plan for our lives.

Gentleness or Meekness

Jesus displayed faithfulness in every aspect of his relationship with the heavenly Father. He also showed meekness. Meekness is all about "submission to the will of God." The idea is "strength under control." Jesus was not weak, but he was meek. Drescher says, "His humility was simply the surrender of Himself to God."[3] We see the secret of a meek spirit in Jesus. What is it? The secret to meekness is shown when Jesus surrenders his will to the will of the Father. Look at these statements: "The Son can do nothing by himself" (John 5:19); "nor does his word dwell in you, for you do not believe the one he sent" (John 5:38); "I am not here on my own" (John 7:28); "I do nothing on my own" (John 8:28); "I am not seeking glory for myself" (John 8:50); "The words I say to you are not just my own" (John 14:10). Meekness is a conscious surrender to God.

The gentleness Jesus showed in his life came to a climax in the Garden of Gethsemane when he prayed, "Yet not as I will, but as you will" (Matt. 26:39). There we have it! Meekness in full.

Self-control

Jesus' life shows faithfulness and meekness, and it also shows self-control. Self-control means "power held in." Remember Jesus when he went before Pontius Pilate. Pilate tried to badger Jesus. Jesus didn't take the bait. Pilate blurted out, "I have power" (John 19:10). Jesus calmly responded, "you would have no power over me if it were not given to you from above" (John 19:11a).

Jesus had many opportunities to lose his control. People insulted him at his trial. The whip lashed his back, yet he kept self-control. How did he do it? Jesus had self-control because he placed himself under the control of the heavenly Father. Jesus demonstrated self-control in full.

How are we supposed to develop this trait? As the life of Jesus is reproduced in us by the Holy Spirit, we can learn to live totally committed to the Lord.

Think about it like this. When the Holy Spirit produces the nine fruit of the Spirit, he is reproducing Christ in us. So you may ask how can this happen to me? How can I become a man or woman in full?

I read about this boy who had a bantam hen. For some reason, the hen laid only small eggs. So the little boy went to town, purchased a big ostrich egg from the market, and returned home. He showed the large ostrich egg to the little bantam hen and said, "Try harder." But you know, the answer is not to "try harder." The answer is to yield daily to the control of the Holy Spirit. Let me make a suggestion. Try to begin each day with this simple prayer and yield your life to the control of the Holy Spirit. Ask the Holy Spirit to take charge of every area of your life and your being. Yield to him body, soul, and Spirit. Ask him to be in charge of all of the relationships, old and new, in your life. Ask him, in every situation you encounter, to manifest his fruit, the life of Jesus, through you. He will.

Rembrandt, the famous Dutch artist, was asked how he knew when a picture was complete. His reply was, "When it expresses the intent of the artist." Excellent reply. When the Master Artist sees in us the life of Christ and the ninefold expression of the fruit of the Spirit, his intent for us has been accomplished. And that's what SpiritFruit is all about.

NOTES

Chapter 1, "God Among the Orchards"

1. Roger Holmes, *Taylor's Guide to Fruits and Berries* (New York: Houghton Mifflin, 1996), 11.

2. Leland Ryken, James C. Wilhoit, and Tremper Longman III, *Dictionary of Biblical Imagery* (Downers Grove, Ill.: InterVarsity Press, 1998), 2:310–11.

3. Stanley M. Burgess, Gary B. McGee, and Paul H. Alexander, eds., *Dictionary of Pentecostal and Charismatic Movement* (Grand Rapids: Zondervan, 1998), 318.

Chapter 2, "Is There a Pomologist in the House?"

1. John M. Drescher, *Doing What Comes Spiritually* (Scottsdale, Penn.: Herald Press, 1993), 16.

2. Henry Barclay Swete, *The Holy Spirit in the New Testament* (London: Macmillan, 1909), 209.

3. W. A. Criswell, *The Holy Spirit in Today's World* (Grand Rapids: Zondervan, 1996), 238.

4. Roger Holmes, ed., *Taylor's Guide to Fruits and Berries* (New York: Houghton Mifflin, 1996), 418.

5. Lehman Strauss, *The Third Person* (New York: Loizeaux Brothers, 1954), 164.

6. Holmes, 393.

7. Dianne Onstad, *Whole Foods Companion* (White River Junction, Vt.: Chelsea Green Publishing Co., 1996), 13.

8. Ibid.

9. Ibid., 14.

10. Paul Brand, *God's Forever Feast* (Grand Rapids: Discovery House, 1998), 94.

Chapter 3, "Love Apples"

1. Dianne Onstad, *Whole Foods Companion* (White River Junction, Vt.: Chelsea Green Publishing Co., 1996), 17–18.

2. Ibid., 18.

3. William Barclay, *The Letters to the Galatians and Ephesians* (Philadelphia: Westminster Press, 1958), 54.

4. Ibid.

5. D. Stuart Briscoe, *Spirit Life* (Old Tappan, N.J.: Fleming H. Revell, 1983), 33.

6. C. S. Lewis, *The Four Loves* (New York: Harcourt, Brace and World, 1960), 176.

7. Timothy George, *The New American Commentary: Galatians* (Nashville: Broadman & Holman, 1994), 401.

8. John M. Drescher, *Doing What Comes Spiritually* (Scottsdale, Penn.: Herald Press, 1993), 99.

9. Ron Hembree, *Fruit of the Spirit* (Grand Rapids: Spire, 1969), 25–26.

10. Drescher, 72.

Chapter 4, "Just Peachy!"

1. Dianne Onstad, *Whole Foods Companion* (White River Junction, Vt.: Chelsea Green Publishing Co., 1996), 109.

2. John M. Drescher, *Doing What Comes Spiritually* (Scottsdale, Penn.: Herald Press, 1993), 91.

3. D. Stuart Briscoe, *Spirit Life* (Old Tappan, N.J.: Fleming H. Revell, 1983), 35–37.

4. William Barclay, *The Letters to the Galatians and Ephesians* (Philadelphia: Westminster Press, 1958), 52.

5. Drescher, 95.

6. Briscoe, 43.

7. Drescher, 81.

8. Ibid., 77.

9. Quoted in ibid., 79.

10. Ron Hembree, *Fruit of the Spirit* (Grand Rapids: Spire, 1969), 32.

11. Drescher, 30.

12. Ibid., 82.

13. Ibid., 89.

Chapter 5, "A Fresh Slice of Peace"

1. Dianne Onstad, *Whole Foods Companion* (White River Junction, Vt.: Chelsea Green Publishing Co., 1996), 143–44.

2. William Barclay, *The Letters to the Galatians and Ephesians* (Philadelphia: Westminster Press, 1958), 55.

3. Eugene H. Peterson, *Traveling Light* (Colorado Springs: Helmers and Howard, 1988), 165.

4. J. Oswald Sanders, *The Holy Spirit and His Gifts* (Grand Rapids: Zondervan, 1970).

5. Timothy George, *The New American Commentary: Galatians* (Nashville: Broadman & Holman, 1994), 402.

6. Ron Hembree, *Fruit of the Spirit* (Grand Rapids: Spire, 1969), 45.

7. Ibid., 45–56.

8. George, 402.

9. John M. Drescher, *Doing What Comes Spiritually* (Scottsdale, Penn.: Herald Press, 1993), 115.

10. Paul Lee Tann, *Encyclopedia of 7,700 Illustrations* (Rockville, Md.: Assurance Publishers, 1979), 507.

Chapter 6, "Looking for Mr. Sweetbar"

1. Dianne Onstad, *Whole Foods Companion* (White River Junction, Vt.: Chelsea Green Publishing Co., 1996), 55–56.

2. William Barclay, *The Letters to the Galatians and Ephesians* (Philadelphia: Westminster Press, 1958), 55.

3. D. Stuart Briscoe, *Spirit Life* (Old Tapan, N.J.: Fleming H. Revell, 1983), 70.

4. W. A. Criswell, *The Holy Spirit in Today's World* (Grand Rapids: Zondervan, 1996), 24.

5. Barclay, 56.

6. Ron Hembree, *Fruit of the Spirit* (Grand Rapids: Spire, 1969), 55.

7. Timothy George, *The New American Commentary: Galatians* (Nashville: Broadman & Holman, 1994), 42.

8. Barclay, 55.

9. John M. Drescher, *Doing What Comes Spiritually* (Scottsdale, Penn.: Herald Press, 1993), 161.

10. Ibid., 165.

11. Ibid., 174.

12. Ibid., 179–80.

13. Ibid., 176.

Chapter 7, "Is Kindness Really All That?"

1. Dianne Onstad, *Whole Foods Companion* (White River Junction, Vt.: Chelsea Green Publishing Co., 1996), 63–64.

2. D. Stuart Briscoe, *Spirit Life* (Old Tappan, N.J.: Fleming H. Revell, 1983), 95.

3. John M. Drescher, *Doing What Comes Spiritually* (Scottsdale, Penn.: Herald Press, 1993), 183.

4. Briscoe, 84.

5. William Barclay, *The Letters to the Galatians and Ephesians* (Philadelphia: Westminster Press, 1958), 56.

6. Drescher, 183.

7. Ron Hembree, *Fruit of the Spirit* (Grand Rapids: Spire, 1969), 66.

8. Drescher, 184.

9. Ibid., 185.

10. Ibid., 191.

11. Ibid., 202.

12. Ibid., 191.

13. Briscoe, 94.

14. Drescher, 201.

15. Hembree, 74.

16. Ibid., 71.

17. Briscoe, 94.

Chapter 8, "The Grapes of Goodness"

1. John Steinbeck, *The Grapes of Wrath*, chapter 25.

2. Leland Ryken, James C. Wilhoit, and Tremper Longman III, *Dictionary of Biblical Imagery* (Downers Grove, Ill.: InterVarsity Press, 1998), 2:310, 348.

3. Dianne Onstad, *Whole Foods Companion* (White River Junction, Vt.: Chelsea Green Publishing Co., 1996), 67–71.

4. Lehman Strauss, *The Third Person* (New York: Loizeaux Brothers, 1954), 110–11.

5. James Henry Thayer, *Greek-English Lexicon of the New Testament* (Grand Rapids: Zondervan, 1963), 3.

6. J. Oswald Sanders, *The Holy Spirit and His Gifts* (Grand Rapids: Zondervan, 1970), 149.

7. Quoted by John M. Drescher in *Doing What Comes Spiritually* (Scottsdale, Penn.: Herald Press, 1993), 209.

8. Ibid., 219.

Chapter 9, "A-Peeling Faithfulness"

1. Dianne Onstad, *Whole Foods Companion* (White River Junction, Vt.: Chelsea Green Publishing Co., 1996), 28–31.

2. William Barclay, *The Letters to the Galatians and Ephesians* (Philadelphia: Westminster Press, 1958), 56.

3. John M. Drescher, *Doing What Comes Spiritually* (Scottsdale, Penn.: Herald Press, 1993), 237.

4. Eugene H. Peterson, *Traveling Light* (Colorado Springs: Helmers and Howard, 1988), 165.

5. Timothy George, *Faithful Witness: The Life and Mission of William Carey* (Birmingham, Ala.: New Hope, 1991), 404.

6. Drescher, 253.

Chapter 10, "Peek Meekness"

1. Dianne Onstad, *Whole Foods Companion* (White River Junction, Vt.: Chelsea Green Publishing Co., 1996), 135–36.

2. William Barclay, *The Letters to the Galatians and Ephesians* (Philadelphia: Westminster Press, 1958), 56–57.

3. J. Oswald Sanders, *The Holy Spirit and His Gifts* (Grand Rapids: Zondervan, 1970), 151.

4. Timothy George, *The New American Commentary: Galatians* (Nashville: Broadman & Holman, 1994), 404.

5. John M. Drescher, *Doing What Comes Spiritually* (Scottsdale, Penn.: Herald Press, 1993), 272

6. George, 404

7. D. Stuart Briscoe, *Spirit Life* (Old Tappan, N.J.: Fleming H. Revell, 1983), 135.

Chapter 11, "Apropos Apricot"

1. Dianne Onstad, *Whole Foods Companion* (White River Junction, Vt.: Chelsea Green Publishing Co., 1996), 25–26.

2. William Barclay, *The Letters to the Galatians and Ephesians* (Philadelphia: Westminster Press, 1958), 57.

3. Timothy George, *The New American Commentary: Galatians* (Nashville: Broadman & Holman, 1994), 404.

4. Eugene H. Peterson, *Traveling Light* (Colorado Springs: Helmers and Howard, 1988), 166.

5. D. Stuart Briscoe, *Spirit Life* (Old Tappan, N.J.: Fleming H. Revell, 1983), 138–140.

6. J. Oswald Sanders, *The Holy Spirit and His Gifts* (Grand Rapids: Zondervan, 1970), 152.

7. John M. Drescher, *Doing What Comes Spiritually* (Scottsdale, Penn.: Herald Press, 1993), 311.

8. Ibid., 316.

Chapter 12, "Full of Fruit"

1. D. Stuart Briscoe, *Spirit Life* (Old Tappan, N.J.: Fleming H. Revell, 1983), 13.

2. John M. Drescher, *Doing What Comes Spiritually* (Scottsdale, Penn.: Herald Press, 1993), 231.

3. Ibid., 2, 6, 7.